STAND UP

STAND UP

*How to Flourish
When the Odds
Are Stacked
Against You*

RENÉ BANGLESDORF

NEW YORK

LONDON • NASHVILLE • MELBOURNE • VANCOUVER

STAND UP

How to Flourish When the Odds Are Stacked Against You

© 2019 René Banglesdorf

Published in New York, New York, by Morgan James Publishing. Morgan James is a trademark of Morgan James, LLC. www.MorganJamesPublishing.com

ISBN 9781642791839 paperback
ISBN 9781642791846 case laminate
ISBN 9781642791853 eBook
Library of Congress Control Number: 2018907976

Cover & Interior Design by:
Christopher Kirk
www.GFSstudio.com

All scriptures are from the NIV unless otherwise noted

Also used The Message and NLT

Cover photo by Trey Freeman Photography

Morgan James is a proud partner of Habitat for Humanity Peninsula and Greater Williamsburg. Partners in building since 2006.

Get involved today! Visit
MorganJamesPublishing.com/giving-back

Table of Contents

Foreword by Jackie Green vii

Introduction: Learning How to Stand Up 1

Chapter 1:   Making Choices. 5

Chapter 2:   Surrendering Unforgiveness 23

Chapter 3:   Planning for Success 35

Chapter 4:   Fulfilling your Destiny. 51

Chapter 5:   Recovering from Failure 67

Chapter 6:   Restoring Harmony 81

Chapter 7:   Handling Hypocrisy. 99

Chapter 8:   Aligning your Future 115

Chapter 9:   Conquering Fears. 129

Chapter 10:   Finding Purpose. 139

About the Author 155

Endnotes. 157

Foreword

There is a time for everything, and a season for
every activity under the heavens: a time to be born
and a time to die... a time to tear down and a time
to build... a time to be silent and a time to speak...
(Eccl. 3:1-3, 7)

Never in my life has so much changed in such a short amount of time. For multiple generations, faith has been very important to our family. But never more than in 2012 when we were faced with decisions that we never anticipated. Because of our deeply held belief we felt we had no choice but to take a stand.

Under provisions of the Affordable Care Act—which passed and was signed into law in 2010 and phased into effect over the next few years—businesses above a certain size in the United States (like Hobby Lobby) were required to provide insurance that covered twenty different forms of contraception. Among these twenty contraception methods were four that were potentially life-terminating drugs and devices. The Federal Department of Health and

Human Services began enforcing this mandate in 2012. Businesses that failed to comply with these requirements faced potentially millions of dollars in fines to the IRS.

This requirement created a moral dilemma for us at Hobby Lobby, and for hundreds, perhaps thousands, of other closely held companies owned by people of faith with pro-life convictions. For our part, we knew in our hearts that we were going to have to take a stand. We also knew that such a stand might mean the crippling or even dismantling of the business that David and Barbara Green, along with our family and others, had poured their lives and hearts into for more than four decades. We also felt the weight of responsibility to the more than thirty-five thousand employees we'd always tried to do right by.

The decision resulted in a two-year legal battle ending with a US Supreme Court ruling in our favor. It also produced opposition, and more importantly, a tremendous outpouring of public and private support, with people all over the world praying for us.

Today, an enlarged photo of our extended family walking down the icy steps of the Supreme Court Building hangs in the conference room of our Family Legacy Center in Oklahoma City as a reminder that prayer, faith, and family unity can carry us through any adversity and create a positive legacy, not just for our family but also for families of faith and conscience all over the nation.

Our stance as stakeholders in Hobby Lobby was a time to tear down, challenging laws that contradicted what we believe is foundational to our nation and the freedom to pursue life and liberty. This time to tear down coincided with a time to build—just one mile away from the Supreme Court Building. In 2012, as our legal battle began, we also acquired property in Washington, DC, just three blocks from the US Capitol to begin building what is now a 430,000-square-foot Museum of the Bible, focusing on the history and cultural significance of the best-selling book of all time.

The public relations and fundraising efforts required to make the dream of the museum a reality also pulled me out of my comfort zone, as I chose to join my husband Steve in an increasing number of public forums and on stages all over the world. As I traded philanthropic ventures closer to home for one that put a microphone in my hand, I began to realize we live in an unprecedented time to speak.

Dr. Martin Luther King, Jr. once said, "Our lives begin to end the day we become silent about things that matter." In an age when right has been declared wrong and human rights are blurred, we all must answer the call to use our voices, reinvest in our communities, and shape our eternal legacy.

We only have one life to live. My prayer is that yours makes the biggest impact for good that it can. I invite you to join René in the coming pages to rise to the challenge to stand up, overcome obstacles and differences, and change your slice of history. And if you need some inspiration along the way, you might find it in the ever-changing exhibits at Museum of the Bible in Washington, DC.

My favorite artifact at Museum of the Bible illustrates a personal legacy of which I am both honored and humbled to be a part. *The Hours and Psalter of Elizabeth de Bohun*, was at one time a centerpiece of the private collection of William Waldorf Astor and heralded by the *Chicago Tribune* as "the grandest 14th Century English manuscript in private hands." This extraordinary manuscript had quite a story behind it that came as a wonderful surprise to me.

In tracing my ancestry over the years, I have discovered familial ties to the first Queen Elizabeth, who reigned from 1558 to 1603, and, her ancestor, Elizabeth de Bohun, who was an English noblewoman and my great grandmother (with 20 more "greats" in front of her name). De Bohun lived only a brief life, yet here we are seven centuries later talking about how her/my family invested our resources in the Word of God. She and her husband commissioned the beautifully illustrated manuscript—at great financial expense—during a time when there was much unrest in England and much of the population could not read.

You never know what your contributions, large or small, will inspire in the future. How are you shaping your legacy?

Jackie Green

Acknowledgements

Many people have helped in my journey to stand up. My Nana diligently taught me about our family, Christians who fled to America from Europe to pursue life, liberty and happiness. Through the years, those same pursuits laid the foundation for my grandparents and parents to model excellence for me. Legacy matters.

In turn, I have tried to model the same excellence for my children, nieces and nephews, and the others whose lives I've had the opportunity to shape. Jake, I've loved you the longest. Thanks for having patience with me as I learned at a young age to be a parent. You certainly made it easy. Brooke, you are my sunshine. I am so proud of you. And Kate, my daughter-in-love, thanks for changing my life forever by making me a grandparent!

Meredith, Eric, Lauren, Kayla, Grant, Zach, John, Emily, Alec, Elijah, Grace, Taylor, Grey, Simone, Lena, Lily, Jameson, Aaron, Jaxson, Olivia, Isaac and Eli—you all inspire me every day. Thanks for listening to my advice, solicited or not, because your responses have shaped my outlook on life and made it richer. It is your generations that make leaving a legacy worthwhile.

Mom, you've faithfully taught me about the importance of treating people well, loving Jesus, and cherishing family. Amy, you've been my lifeline ever since long distance calls ceased to be billed by the minute—and my beloved sister since the day you rocked my three-year-old life.

Karen, thank you for pushing me to put pen to paper to tell how faith infused my journey. Larry, my writing skills flourished under your tutelage and encouragement, both equally important. Steve, I appreciate your diligence in reshaping my theme and helping develop my "why." To my friends over the years, I would still be in my shell if not for your prodding and cheering. Thank you.

I'd also like to extend my appreciation to those in the aviation industry who have welcomed, educated and encouraged my professional pursuits. My fellow board members in the International Aviation Women's Association, you've inspired me. Thanks also to my team at Charlie Bravo Aviation—especially Jennifer, for keeping all the details straight, and Keith, for listening, reading and proofing it all.

Curt, God knew what He was doing when He put the two of us together. You have believed in me. You have invested in me. You have pushed me out of my comfort zone more than you know. Thank you for letting me pursue my dreams, and for being the kind of man who is not intimidated by a successful woman.

Jesus, I cannot get through a day without you. Thank you for loving me beyond measure. Thank you for the gift of words. May I live my life using them wisely.

Introduction

Learning How to Stand Up

My childhood started like most everyone else's. I was blessed with two arms and two legs. Ten fingers and ten toes. A few months after I was born, my mom, a nursing student, noticed that my hip joints didn't move correctly and reached out to a pediatrician. I ended up the recipient of metal leg braces, courtesy of the Shriners Hospital in Atlanta, Georgia. I'm told I wore them for most of my first year of life, and let me tell you, I am thankful I can't remember that.

Those braces—and the trials, perseverance and faith they produced—are what gave me the foundation on which I stand today. I just didn't see it as it was happening. Isn't that the way of life? When we look back, our perspective grows and gives us a different hope for the future. Oftentimes, examining our survival illuminates an opportunity to help others.

That is the impetus for this book. I strongly believe women, all women—conservative and liberal alike— stand on the cusp of an opportunity to inspire change in the world around us and climb to new heights, pursuing our own dreams and legacies. On the heels of a woman running for president of the United States, an outcry for women's rights around the world, and the unprecedented exposure of sexual abuse and harassment in every industry, the time to evoke change is now.

We have the opportunity—no, obligation—to not just lean in but to *stand up*. Standing is a posture of leadership and readiness. Standing up means that we move into a role. We quit making excuses or blaming others. We find our voice. We use our influence. We confront bullies and bickering. We defy the status quo.

I am not claiming to have it all figured out. I have by no means "arrived." I've heard courage is pressing through fear and doing something daring anyway. That's where I am. I've taken the long, hard road to get here, and I sincerely hope by sharing my story, I'll somehow encourage you to stand up, too. Because just when you get there, I'm probably going to need some more encouragement on my journey. We need each other.

Today, I'm a trailblazer in the aviation industry. I operate in a 99 percent male-dominated role: selling private jets. I've climbed some boulders, faced down discrimination, fallen flat on my face, and pulled myself back up again more times than I can count. I've had my very own #metoo story, I've nearly died a few times, and I've rebuilt a dream after dropping out of college to abruptly start a family.

Through it all—and sometimes when I didn't even recognize it—the foundation of my childhood trials and faith has sustained me. Maybe you have a faith journey like mine. Maybe you don't even know what that is. Either way, I think you'll find nuggets of wisdom and encouragement in my experiences.

I've included how my faith fits into my everyday life because on the darkest days, I found solace in the stories and the words of the Bible. In knowing that those who went before me often faced bigger obstacles, more dire circumstances, and without knowing it, far greater opportunities for impact. I can't imagine that many of them knew their stories would inspire billions of people hundreds of generations later.

The same is true for us. Our faithfulness in the seemingly little things today may have impact beyond our limited human comprehension. And the failure to engage those muscles, the talents we have been given, conversely could cost more than we could ever imagine. Now is the time to dig in. Make a difference. Take a chance. Stand up. I believe we are stronger standing together, and I'm so honored to join you.

Chapter 1

Making Choices

T aking a stand, exposing an atrocity, or pointing out an injustice should be applauded. But the real change comes not from the identification of the problem, but from the resulting solution. With the explosion of social media, gossip presented as news, and the #metoo movement, opportunities to attack others have exploded.

The opportunities to exhibit grace also have expanded exponentially.

My mama told me when I was little that if I didn't have anything nice to say, not to say anything at all. There are a few politicians I wish had learned that lesson. Shoot, sometimes I wish I had listened to it better.

I say things I regret.

I also do things I regret.

Those things can have far-reaching consequences— something the sometimes-unsavory characters in the Bible experienced.

How we handle our choices matters.

This may be hard for you to read. You may have had choices made for you that violated you, demeaned you, destroyed your dreams or devastated your family. My intention is not to revisit your hurts but instead to show you how I progressed past my own rough experience.

I was date-raped in college.

There. I said it. I tried to think of a way to sugarcoat it, but that approach just seemed to contradict the brutality of the act. I can say it now without reliving it, which is a good thing. My prayer is that if you've also been a victim, you will be able to talk about it someday without terror or shame. I so admire the women I've heard speak about their experiences being trafficked and emotionally broken, who have been able to put their lives and dignity back together over time. It gives me hope for you no matter what you've experienced.

Please know I believe no behavior that violates another person is acceptable. And how I've chosen to handle my situation casts no judgement on how you work through yours. My prayer is that my vulnerability can help you make successive choices to move on with your life.

The night it happened, I was not in the library studying. I was not walking between classes in the dark. I was in a bar, underaged, allowing a hunky hockey player to buy me a drink, an amaretto sour. The perfect drink to drug because of the open container and mixed flavors.

I remember compliantly walking out of the bar with him. I have flashbacks of a beanbag chair in a dorm room. I remember him walking me back into the bar and depositing me with my friends, whom he told I had too much to drink.

When I awakened the next morning, fuzzy-headed and nauseous, I discovered bruises in places bruises shouldn't be. I surmised what happened the night before, which was later confirmed through snide comments from the man's roommate, who found it entertaining.

I felt like an idiot, embarrassed, and ashamed of myself. I didn't report it. It is only now, when I see young women drinking themselves into oblivion, that I speak up. If I had not been breaking the law, using a fake ID to get into a bar and drinking underage, the likelihood of an incident like that would have decreased drastically.

I did not deserve to be raped. Nobody does. But I certainly didn't do everything I could have to prevent the crime.

I chose not to report the rape. Mostly because of shame. Thirty years later, and no longer dealing with any of those emotions, I have no desire to prosecute or dredge up hard feelings. My way of dealing with this is my own. I have not walked in anyone else's shoes. Assuredly I didn't bring this up so I could say #metoo.

Going forward in each of our stories, we must not put ourselves purposefully into situations where our discernment is challenged, our defenses are weakened, or our paths can be distorted by someone else. If we want to leave a legacy of excellence, we must be on guard. We must set goals and plan for the future.

In Romans, Paul tells us, "don't become so well-adjusted to your culture that you fit into it without even thinking. Instead fix your attention on God. You'll be changed from the inside out. Readily recognize what He wants from you and quickly respond to it. Unlike the culture around you, always dragging you down to its level of immaturity, God brings the best out of you, develops well-formed maturity in you" (Rom 12:2, MSG).

I want that. I want it for me and for you. For my daughter and daughter-in-law and sisters and nieces and everyone whose path crosses mine. I want people to see the best in me and you.

Interacting with God's Word everyday gives us the fortitude to say no to poor decisions more often. Reading it, quoting it, praying it, singing it, memorizing it, using it to instruct or encourage others, questioning it, and meditating on it enables us to choose the right thing more often.

Avoid Vulnerable Situations

My rape in college was not the first time my choices put me in harm's way. I was twelve the first time my life flashed before my eyes. My mom had allowed me to go with a friend's family to Lake Erie. My friend and I, feeling pretty independent, grabbed a raft—actually a four-foot by eight-foot by two-foot chunk of Styrofoam—and set out to get a tan on the water. We were chatting away about boys and parents, not paying attention to our surroundings. When we looked up and could barely see the shore, we realized the wind was blowing our makeshift raft rapidly away from land.

The logical next step in our adolescent minds was to abandon ship and swim back to shore. The one we could barely see.

After swimming for as long as we could, treading water, floating, and yes, even praying, a rowboat appeared. Two fishermen dragged our waterlogged bodies aboard and motored us back to the dock.

How they found us or knew where we needed to go, I'll never know this side of heaven. In retrospect, there were some life lessons to be learned from my near-drowning.

We can drift away from where we are supposed to be without even realizing it. And our next decisions can cause us to abandon the thing that will keep us from dying—spiritually, emotionally or physically. Each one of us has something in our lives that keeps us from the extraordinary, victorious, dream life we want. Nobody likes to talk about sin, secret vices, moral failures, or whatever you like to call it. But how we handle these variances makes the difference between mediocrity and excellence in our lives.

The opportunities to make bad decisions hit us from all directions. We can be drawn to illegal or immoral actions, like stealing from an employer, lying for a friend, or having an affair. But we also can fall into withholding our best efforts, conforming to societies' less-than-ideal norms, or settling for mediocrity.

In an age where we can examine infinite possibilities and get nearly anything we want instantly—or at least with two-day free shipping—we face temptation more than ever before. While everyone is different, how we handle some common things can make all the difference in our lives.

Beware Comparison

I can't help it. It just happens. I compare prices. Fruit colors at the grocery store. The length of my hair with the photo that was taken six months ago. Which eye has more wrinkles around it. My tendency to size things up is endless. No matter when in my life I've taken the Myers Briggs personality assessment, I always end up with a J (for judgment), even when other letters have changed.

This constant analysis, assessment and appropriation helps me to process information and make good decisions. It can also make me critical and judgmental. And at its worst, this tendency pushes me into jealousy or insecurity.

Early in my marriage I hated going to social events with my husband Curt. I've mostly been an introvert throughout my life. My husband thrives around people and rarely needs downtime. In almost every situation, he's the life of the party. While he enjoyed being in the spotlight, I felt ignored and insignificant. I remember thinking I had things to offer, too, and wondering why people didn't pay attention to me.

Today, I can appreciate him getting his fill of attention from other people, letting me spend time getting to know others one-on-one. I've learned he has his part to play, and I have mine. If we were the same, we wouldn't offer each other the balance we do now. It sounds silly to be jealous of my husband being the DJ at a party, but it happened for years. Now I'm glad when he's in charge of what's playing from the speakers. He's good at reading a crowd and playing music they like. I'm happy to celebrate his song-picking prowess, because it means everyone has more fun. I barely change my radio station. I would hate that pressure.

When my kids were younger, I thought I wanted them to become collegiate athletes. I compared their skills to other kids'. Boasted about their grades and vertical jump and every other thing a parent can be tempted into comparing. But neither of them decided to play competitive sports beyond high school. Now after watching my sister-in-law handle my six-foot-ten nephew's Division I basketball scholarship offers and college athletic career, I'm thankful they made the choice that they did.

We need to keep in mind we don't know the struggles and the sacrifices on the flip side of others' success. Perhaps we wouldn't want to pay the price. Maybe it looks good on them, but it wouldn't fit us the same— whatever "it" is.

I've learned to be comfortable saying "good for them," even when I have to shush the little voice that whispers "why don't I have that?" The temptation to feed jealousy and insecurity lessens when I reflect on the things for which I am grateful, like good health, a career I enjoy, and a home in Texas.

In her book *Why Her? 6 Truths We Need to Hear When Measuring Up Leaves Us Falling Behind*, Nicki Koziarz admits:

Comparison can sneak into my heart no matter how strong my level of gratefulness and awareness. But by taking the time to recognize and thank God for the blessings He puts into my life each day—by taking a good, holy, healthy kind of pride in my current situation—I'm much more able to stay honest and content with who I am and who I'm not. Staring too long at the success of someone else can make us miss our own satisfaction with life.[1]

Avoid Areas of Compromise

I have a big sweet tooth. Maybe I should say all of my teeth are sweet. When I am trying to avoid sugar because it gives me zits, sugar crashes and gut issues, I don't even drive down the street where Dunkin Donuts sits. I take the other way. I know what to do—I steer clear of the things that will lead me into temptation. The wisdom is there, even when the discipline isn't. I say that because I still give in to sugar cravings sometimes.

The consequences of occasionally splurging on sweets are minimal, but there are areas where any compromise can be devastating. However, like I do with my donut detours, we can put safeguards in place.

In the spring of 2017, several media outlets criticized Vice President Mike Pence's stance on not eating alone with women other than his wife. This was triggered by a *Washington Post* article disclosing the practice.[2] He was charged with being old-fashioned and worse, but I find his ideals refreshing. I think he honors his wife and other women by not putting them in a compromising position.

Ironically, following this discourse around the vice president's practices, there appeared a tidal wave of exposés on celebrities, politicians and businessmen who had taken advantage of coworkers or subordinates. Makes the VP look wise, doesn't it? Especially as some of the cases were found to be exaggerated for political reasons.

That same year, we saw a drastic increase in the number of reported sexual harassment incidents. Many offenders' careers and lives were destroyed. And I can almost guarantee that for every one exposed, another ten or twenty are still held secret. I don't know a single woman who has not been touched or spoken to inappropriately at some point in her life. I'm thankful we're talking about the wrongs, and I'm glad perpetrators are being forced to think twice about acting inappropriately.

While we don't invite this kind of abuse, like my story earlier, sometimes we put ourselves in a situation that makes it easier for someone else to misbehave.

We Must Use the Weapons We Have

If we want to be powerful, truth is one of the strongest weapons we can wield. The Hazelden Betty Ford Foundation purports, "Looking in the mirror and accepting what we see can be one of the hardest things we ever do. It's especially hard when the image staring us in the face is painful or doesn't fit with how we want to see ourselves. Sometimes, the truth is painful and we avoid it at any cost. Refusing to accept a painful reality that alters the perception of ourselves is a psychological defense called denial."[3]

Addicted people don't have a monopoly on denial. For years, I used my introversion as an excuse not to reach out and be a good friend or neighbor. But being a hermit because it's easier and because people are messy and needy does not make the world a better place. If I am truthful with myself, I know I need to be a friend to have friends, and I must come out of my comfort zone if I want to leave an impactful and lasting legacy.

If the first weapon is truth, weapon number two is love.

While he was in jail for non-violent protest in 1967, Dr. Martin Luther King, Jr. wrote a speech about loving your enemies. The speech included his famous quote, "Darkness cannot drive out darkness: only light can do that. Hate cannot drive out hate: only love can do that."

Fast forward fifty years to the 2016 US presidential election. I cannot find any documentation indicating the democratic process was designed to be hateful. But hateful it was. The United States experienced a surge in hate crime in the ten days after Donald Trump was elected president, according to a report from the Southern Poverty Law Center.[4]

People "unfriending" or "unfollowing" others on social media gained national media attention. Research from the American Psychological Association indicated political discussions at work caused stress and reduced productivity.[5]

My extended family members, who normally love discussing politics and current events, declared the

Thanksgiving following the election to be a political-discussion-free holiday so familial love could be restored among those with opposing viewpoints. Our love for one another had to trump dissention to keep our family intact. I wish more families took this approach then, as I hear of many still reeling from the discord.

If there's a silver lining in storm clouds, I witnessed it in 2017. I saw a restored sense of community stirred up in the hurricane clouds that hovered over Texas, Louisiana, Florida, Puerto Rico and much of the Caribbean late in the summer of 2017. Channels that fostered talk of hate turned to rally cries to help fellow Texans, then all Americans and others affected by the historic storms. My heart was warmed watching the growth of the Cajun Navy, informal ad-hoc volunteer groups comprised of private boat owners who assisted law enforcement in rescuing tens of thousands of citizens.

In my own community, I connected church and neighborhood resources with concerned aircraft owners. Working with my friends Robin Eissler and Eileen Minogue, and their Sky Hope Network, in five days we were able to transport more than 200,000 pounds of relief supplies by air on small private planes into areas inaccessible by road.

Friends and neighbors showed up in droves at the hangar where we staged operations. On Saturday, we had more than 120 volunteers receiving, organizing, weighing, and loading supplies. They came in response to posts they'd seen on the same social media outlets that weeks before were overflowing with malicious and destructive sentiments.

Love thwarts hate. Love defeats cynicism. And 1 Peter 4:8 tells us love covers a multitude of sins. It is a powerful weapon.

Our most powerful resource, however, is weapon number three: prayer.

Jesus told his disciples to "watch and pray" (Matt. 26:41) and to "get up and pray" (Luke 22:46) so they would not fall into temptation. The Bible frequently shows Jesus going away by himself to pray, setting the example for prayer's vital importance. There's nothing more offensive to Satan than using God's own words.

When Jesus was tempted by Satan to turn a stone into a loaf of bread, He answered with scripture. "It is written, 'Man shall not live by bread alone, but by every word that comes from the mouth of God'" (Matt. 4:4). Later, when the disciples asked Jesus to teach them how to pray, he mentioned bread again, telling them to ask God for their daily bread. If we cannot live by bread alone, then we also must ask for spiritual provision. Daily.

The Bible is rich with promises we can pray and claim. I encourage you to get to know them. Resources abound to help with this strategy. Several powerful women have fueled my prayer life with their instruction. Stormie Omartian's *The Power of a Praying Wife* and subsequent related titles, and Beth Moore's *Praying God's Word* have taught me more than I could relay in an entire book, let alone a section of a chapter.

Focus on the Reward for Choosing Right

Besides the natural consequences of clean living, we face spiritual implications as well. God rewards doing right. Some of my favorite verses about obedience and the resulting blessings sit at the beginning of Deuteronomy 28. I personalize the passage a bit, since having blessings in my herds and flocks doesn't mean much to me. When I paraphrase it for myself, it goes more like this.

If I obey the Lord my God and carefully keep his commands, my town and neighborhood will be blessed. My children and their families will be blessed. My business and employees will be blessed. My sales and marketing efforts will be blessed. Wherever I go and whatever I do, I will be blessed. The Lord will conquer my enemies when they attack me. The Lord will guarantee a blessing on everything I do and will fill my storehouses with plenty. He will bless me in the territory He is assigning me.

If I obey the commands of the Lord my God and walk in His ways, the Lord will establish me as His holy daughter, and everyone with whom I come into contact will see that I am different, blessed by the Lord. He will give me prosperity, blessing me with people to mentor, affluent businesses, and sound investments. The Lord will send what I need at the proper time and will bless all the work I do. I will lend to many but need to borrow from none.

If I am sensitive to the commands of the Lord my God and carefully obey them, He will make me the head and not the tail. I will be at the top of my game and never skulking around the bottom.

I challenge you to read Deuteronomy 28 and personalize it. The promises are powerful—for obedience and disobedience.

Besides heavenly blessings, another benefit of staying on a straight path is inner peace. When we tell the truth, we don't have to keep up with which lies we've told to whom. When we say no to doing something we know is bad, we are not consumed with guilt and shame. We can follow a clear direction when we attempt to please God instead of falling subject to others' feelings when we seek the approval of people.

Twelve-step programs born out of Alcoholics Anonymous stress the importance of honesty. Lying and dishonesty are prevalent character defects in all addicts. Those who follow their program learn a new way of life, and a freedom that comes with their change in behavior.

For me, my greatest reward is just that—honesty. I am able to look into the mirror and like the person I see underneath my skin. Ultimately this helps me overcome my lack of belief in myself. Self-worth is something I feed every day with intentional actions and measured reactions. I'm still not there, but I am going in the right direction.

We Must Stand Firm

I try to stand firm in what I believe. Many times, I succeed, but occasionally, I fail. I find when I do succeed, the impetus was resolve, a determination to follow through with something I already decided. One of my favorite "aha" moments occurred when I found some fellows who did the same.

A handful of teenage boys who lived centuries ago made a profound impact on history. They started with decisions about what to eat and not eat. Daniel and his countrymen, Hananiah, Mishael, and Azariah, were selected for special training with the Chaldeans so they could serve King Nebuchadnezzar. Perhaps you know Daniel's friends better as Shadrach, Meshach and Abednego.

They asked to eat according to the diet from God they followed instead of the rich fare provided by the King— and they were honored for it with God's favor. Later in their lives, they were asked to kneel before another god, an idol. They chose to stand firm. Probably as late teenagers. In a foreign, hostile culture.

Those boys did not get there, then decide among themselves not to bow. That decision was made in the early days of their servitude to King Nebuchadnezzar when they chose to follow their God in obedience with the foods the Jewish religion allowed and prohibited.

The consequences for disobeying the king were dire, much worse than a profusion of negative social media responses or being fired unjustly. When the king heard of their rebellion, he summoned them. He told them he would give them another chance to bow and cued the orchestra. The three young men still stood. Unflinching.

Nebuchadnezzar threatened, "If you do not worship [the image], you will be thrown immediately into a blazing furnace. Then what god will be able to rescue you from my hand?"

Shadrach, Meshach and Abednego replied, "King Nebuchadnezzar, we do not need to defend ourselves before you in this matter. If we are thrown into the blazing furnace, the God we serve is able to deliver us from it, and he will deliver us from Your Majesty's hand. But even if he does not, we want you to know, Your Majesty, that we will not serve your gods or worship the image of gold you have set up" (Dan. 3:16).

Bold. Unwavering. *Predetermined* decision.

Again, Shadrach, Meshach and Abednego were rewarded. These men walked in the fire with the Lord—and came out unsinged. The king decreed nobody could say anything against their God, and he promoted them. Profound repercussions like that change the course of history.

This kind of obedience and favor is not a spur-of-the-moment decision, but rather a lifetime of choosing right. When we make the right choices in the little things, sticking with them is easier as the choices become more monumental.

We succeed in standing strong against temptation when we protect ourselves where we are weak. We flourish when we keep our focus on our strengths and blessings instead of wanting to stand in someone else's shoes, when we know and use the weapons we have, when we protect ourselves from vulnerabilities. We triumph when we hold our resolve about the most important things.

In the meantime, we should give ourselves a little grace to become stronger one step, one day at a time. We don't become perfect overnight (or ever, for that matter). And we certainly continue to fail from time to time.

True confession about my sugar addiction. As I sit here writing, I haven't eaten a donut in months. My coffee is black and unsweetened. However, just last week, I succumbed to the need for the nine-dollar bag of peanut M&Ms in the hotel minibar late at night.

At least it wasn't the Oreos *and* the M&Ms.

Choices matter. What we invite into our lives and what we shun *matters*. How we react to the hard decisions is just as important as what we do in everyday life. Those little things help us make the bigger decisions better. Learn from the past—mine and your own—to write the future you want for yourself.

Chapter 2

Surrendering Unforgiveness

My own experiences aren't the only ones that have shaped the way I live. I have learned a few life lessons from watching others. To this day, my mother is one of the best teachers I have. Her consistency empowers me.

Together with her older and younger brother, my mom had a childhood filled with mistreatment by their alcoholic father. The worst abuse was directed toward my mom, the only girl and a sweet, mild-tempered peacemaker. She was both saddened and relieved when her father left home when she was seventeen.

Then she had the opportunity to start a new life when she moved eight hours away to attend nursing school. Instead of blaming people for the abuse she had endured and playing the victim, she chose a life filled with love, got married, and gave birth to me.

While my maternal grandmother could (and did) hold a grudge for decades, I don't remember my mom ever being resentful or bitter. Instead, she chose to forgive people. She forgave her father for every bad thing he did to her. Eventually, she also forgave her mother for not protecting her.

Through counseling she received years afterward, my mom forgave herself for the feelings of shame that came along with being a victim of abuse. And when I rebelled as a teenager, she grounded me and forgave me for lying… more times than I care to admit.

The ultimate test of her forgiveness came twenty-four years after my mom's nuclear family fell apart. It was two weeks after my son, her first grandchild, was born. Mom received a phone call from a hospital in Spokane, Washington. Her daddy had suffered a series of strokes and she was listed as next of kin on his paperwork.

Knowing a little bit of what he had done to her, I couldn't believe she traveled from Indiana to a Spokane nursing home, not just that once, but twice a year for sixteen years to visit the man who robbed her of a normal childhood. By the time they were reunited, he could barely speak. He couldn't voice any regrets, and my mom never knew if he felt any remorse. But she told him repeatedly that she forgave him.

Throughout my life, my mom showed me—through her actions—that forgiveness meant freedom. By choosing to forgive, she gained liberty to live her life unfettered by the choices others made for her. She never chose to be abused, but she took control of her feelings and chose to forgive.

To move forward emotionally and spiritually, you must understand what other people do is out of your control.

What is in your control is how you will react, and if you will allow those people or situations to hold you back. The ability to forgive is essential for anyone who wants to live for the future and not stay mired in past circumstances.

Forgiveness proves essential in our professional lives as well. We can hold onto bad feelings from slights, like a sarcastic comment during a meeting, or major infractions, like an unwarranted probation. However justified, a bad attitude can squash our chances for promotion. By holding onto offenses, we can get stuck in a cubicle instead of working our way into the corner office.

My mom likes to say, "If you hold onto garbage, you tend to smell like garbage." She means that metaphorically about bad feelings, ugly thoughts, or grudges. But hang onto them and see if people don't give you a wide berth as if you'd been rolling in it.

Forgiving is Not the Same as Forgetting

Forgiving someone does not mean excusing them from consequences. It means we are not allowing the offense— or perceived offense—to shackle us.

Sometimes we confuse forgiving with forgetting, which is putting something behind us and never thinking of it again. The two should not be confused, especially when we still associate with the person who has offended us.

In the instance of my date rape, I did not forget how I got myself into that situation nor the person who took advantage of me. He was in a class with me—and the next year I dated one of his fraternity brothers. In fact, I ended up being that fraternity's sweetheart. But I was never alone with that man again. Didn't engage in conversation. I've never forgotten the betrayal of trust. I learned later this approach is healthy.

Boundaries should be established where infractions have occurred. Boundaries should be secured where offenses have the *potential* to occur.

As parents, we should know what's going on in our kids' lives and create limits and rules and stick by them. The biggest pitfall I see right now in my nieces' and nephews' lives is having their own phone at an early age. It opens up all sorts of opportunities for problems, some of them atrocities committed by or against these young technology gurus.

Having a cell phone is a privilege. It comes with responsibilities—for both parents and kids. Parents need to set age-appropriate restrictions on use, with time limits, application download rules and perhaps a filter, like Net Nanny, which protects kids from accessing certain sites.

When kids break rules, they need consequences. Take the phone away. Let them miss a game, even when their team is counting on them. Allow them to experience failure. This is what helps them understand as they grow older, there are consequences to breaking moral codes and laws.

The same thing applies to adult relationships. When someone hurts us, we need to put measures in place to ensure they cannot fall back into the same pattern and continue to do the same thing to us. We could spend less time with the person, reduce the amount of confidential information shared, or, in the case of infidelity, perhaps have access to that person's personal communications.

These principles also apply in the workplace. We can forgive a boss for overlooking us for a promotion. Yes, that can be tough, but it can be done. Or a co-worker for taking credit for our idea. Or an employee for spewing negativity unfairly. But if we allow it to continue, we miss opportunities to grow.

I've found when I isolate exactly what hurt me, pray about confronting it, and then calmly address the situation, it usually clears up. When I let negative feelings fester, I feed resentment and my job performance falls.

If you are in a workplace where you are underappreciated, underpaid or undermined, nobody says you can't find a new job. However, if you cannot leave behind any bitterness about an old one, you'll bring the same poison into the new position.

Letting Go

I learned the meaning of forgiveness on a hot and humid day when I lived in Northern Virginia. I woke up mad. Furious, actually. I don't remember why, and if I did, it wouldn't matter. I didn't want to feel this angry. I thought I'd try to burn it off. I grabbed my Walkman, shoved in a tape of Michael W. Smith's worship music, and took off on the meandering trails through the lush forest behind my house.

Music pumping and arms pumping harder, I power-walked up and down the rolling hills. I stopped at a downed tree, pressed stop on the cassette player, and sat on the log.

"God, I'm tired of being angry," I prayed. "This is wearing me out."

Let it go.

"I don't think it's that simple, God. I mean, I have a good reason to be angry."

Let it go.

"Okay. I'll try. I'll let it go." I prayed out loud, not caring if the squirrels or the birds or the kids on their scooters heard. The vise of anger squeezing my chest released. I filled my lungs. The weight on my shoulders lifted. I straightened them.

As I began walking again, I chanted under my breath, "I let go. I let go. I let go."

I don't know if anyone else noticed the change in me when I returned home, but my revelation revolutionized my relationship with God—and with others.

I learned forgiveness is as simple as letting go.

We Must Forgive God

Tragedies happen all around us. School and church shootings, acts of hatred and terror, deaths and chronic illnesses in children, abuses and lies and atrocities we cannot begin to imagine. We often cry out to God that He could have prevented them. Some break my heart more than others.

Early in 2018, *The Sun*, a popular UK publication, reported on a dossier delivered to the United Nations in 2017. The report estimates UN aid workers have committed as many as 60,000 rapes in the last decade around the world.[1]

The bombshell dossier was handed over by former senior United Nations official Andrew Macleod to Department for International Development Secretary Priti Patel. In it, Professor Macleod also estimated there are 3,300 pedophiles working for the UN or its agencies. Thousands more "predatory" sex abusers specifically target aid charity jobs to get close to vulnerable women and children.

Imagine being traumatized by losing your home and perhaps your family, being shuffled into a refugee camp and then further victimized by someone extending the only help you can get.

When bad things happen to us, or we hear of someone experiencing the unimaginable, many people ask, why does God allow bad things to happen to good people? Conversely, we also wonder why he allows bad people to have good things or to go unpunished. Outside of an eternal perspective, nobody can answer these questions.

In the context of eternity, the suffering on earth, while no less horrific, becomes a mere speck of time in which we all choose our eternal destiny. God created humans with free will, so they could know the difference between good and evil and hopefully choose good. This all-knowing, all-seeing, all-powerful God has given us a way to have an *eternity* with no suffering and no tears instead of an eternity with only suffering and agony.

Where is God while we are suffering? He is on His throne in heaven, allowing us to decide, in spite of suffering or maybe through the suffering, if we will choose good and follow Him, or if we will reject Him and therefore subject ourselves to eternal suffering.

Oftentimes it is in the suffering that people turn to God. He promises an afterlife, one in which there is no suffering, for those who chose to believe in Him.

If we harbor anger at God for not stopping some atrocity—whether or not it touches us personally—we put our salvation at risk.

We Must Forgive Ourselves

I've made some bad decisions. You probably have too. Many of us live with regret, wishing we would have acted or reacted to something in a different manner. In those situations, remorse, shame or guilt can confine our dreams and expectations like a prison wall. They can limit us from becoming more than what we are right now. Instead of a life filled with great breakthroughs and success after success, the consequences of our choices can pigeonhole us into going through the motions, haunted by our pasts.

We must *forgive* ourselves. If we remain unforgiving toward ourselves, we cheapen what God sent His Son to destroy. Two crippling byproducts of unforgiveness are guilt and shame.

In a *Psychology Today* article, counselor Beverly Engel says:

> Some have explained the difference between shame and guilt as follows: When we feel guilt we feel badly about something we did or neglected to do. When we feel shame we

feel badly about who we are. When we feel guilty we need to learn that it is okay to make mistakes. When we feel shame we need to learn that it is okay to be who we are.

I believe self-forgiveness is the most powerful step you can take to rid yourself of debilitating shame. This is particularly true for those who have been abused, but it applies to everyone. Self-forgiveness is not only recommended but absolutely essential if we wish to become emotionally healthy and have peace of mind. It goes like this: the more shame you heal, the more you will be able to see yourself more clearly—the good and the bad. You will be able to recognize and admit how you have harmed yourself and others. Your relationships with others will change and deepen. More importantly, your relationship with yourself will improve.[2]

Self-forgiveness removes a barrier between who we are and who God created us to be. By processing my mistakes, deciding not to repeat them, and leaving them in the past, I find I have more power to make good decisions in the future.

Practice Forgiving the Little Things

Sometimes the grievances we hold onto are a result of our own unrealistic expectations. This can start in childhood, when we want our parents to meet a silly and impossible dream—like buying a pony for Christmas when living in an inner-city apartment. As adults, we sometimes expect another person to resolve our unhappiness or feelings of insecurity.

We need to be careful about the requirements we put on other people. Self-examination triggers opportunities to forgive little things. Analyzing others' motives also can relieve the burden of unforgiveness.

About the same time as my power-walking revelation in the woods, I heard a simple sermon that's made a powerful impact on my life.

The pastor passed out brown paper bags with a sticker on the front that read: God Bag. It contained blank slips of paper. He instructed the congregation to write down the things we wanted to give to God to handle, including things we worry about and those we needed to forgive.

He suggested that every time we fretted about something or picked an offense back up, instead of letting it fester, we should pluck a slip of paper from the bag, pray over it again, and stick it back in the bag where the God of the universe could attend to it.

Over the years, I've learned the principle and don't need the physical reminder. But that bag admonished me from the top of my refrigerator for years. I cannot claim to be a quick learner on this subject, and I admire those who seem to master it early.

A wise seventeen-year-old named Cassie told me that to forgive the big things, you must forgive the little ones. She's had more to forgive than most adults I know.

At age twelve, Cassie was raped by the senior captain of the high school football team. She pressed charges. Knocking the hometown hero off a pedestal had emotional repercussions. She battled depression, self-loathing, and thoughts of suicide. She bears the scars of cutting herself repeatedly for more than a year.

Two years later, someone close to the family molested her and tried to avoid blame by saying Cassie was having flashbacks of her earlier experience. She tried drugs and battled more self-hatred.

When she was sixteen, she secretly started dating a nineteen-year-old man named Jay, not knowing he really was a twenty-four-year-old named David. After dating him for seven months and even meeting his family, who preserved his fake identity, she discovered messages on his cell phone and learned he was not monogamous.

It turned out David had sexual relations with at least seventeen other young women—many only thirteen or fourteen, and some of whom he was paying to use. Cassie took screenshots, captured logins, and helped put a pedophile in jail.

Shortly after his incarceration, police officers called Cassie's parents to say she needed to be tested for HIV. While Cassie miraculously did not test positive for HIV, she did have other complications that make natural childbearing impossible for her. What she once thought of as a simple act of rebellion—hiding a relationship from her parents—produced a bitter consequence.

But Cassie's wide smile and cheerful outlook as she spoke with me over FaceTime—two days before going to court to testify against David, no less—can teach all of us something. To forgive the big things, you must begin letting go of the trivial ones, like snarky comments or a dirty look.

If there's one sure thing that will keep you down, it's lacking the courage to forgive.

Lewis B. Smedes, a twentieth-century author and philosopher, said, "To forgive is to set a prisoner free and discover that the prisoner was you."[3]

Poet Maya Angelou took the concept a step further. "Bitterness is like a cancer. It eats upon the host."

Don't let unforgiveness eat you alive, make you its prisoner, or hold you back. Success is difficult enough to achieve without carrying all the baggage that bitterness brings.

Chapter 3
Planning for Success

I had big plans as a teenager. I enrolled in one of the best journalism schools in the nation, Ohio University in Athens. I considered myself well on my way to making my dreams come true.

Being a typical overachieving college student, I made good grades and juggled several leadership roles. I was a resident assistant in an upperclassmen's dorm, a senior writer for the school newspaper, and vice president of my sorority. I dreamed of graduating and becoming a top-notch investigative reporter.

On a cloudy day at the beginning of April 1991, the future I envisioned for myself imploded. I walked from my dorm to the local CVS drugstore, checked to see if anyone I knew was there, and bought a home pregnancy test. I darted across the alley to a Wendy's and locked myself in a bathroom stall. I anxiously waited to see if a little pink line would predict my future.

With the positive result, I realized the goals I set for myself were no longer realistic. I got engaged to Curt that day, and before the end of the year was a college dropout, a young wife, and a first-time mother.

However, I was still the same person, with the same strengths and talents. I learned when circumstances derail your plans, you can choose to feel sorry for yourself or make the best of it, pick a new path, and find an alternate form of success. I poured my energy into being a great wife and mother instead of a world-class journalist.

We all must decide to succeed, whether our plans change because of our own choices or something outside of our control. When you feel you're not sure what do next, you might be exactly where you're supposed to be. Whether we feel like it or not, we must pick ourselves up and do the next right thing. Right now.

In those days right after I was married, the responsibilities of being a homemaker and my lack of a degree made it difficult for me to find work as a freelancer in suburban Washington, D.C., where Curt and I had moved for his job. I thought my career dreams were dead. But during those years, new priorities factored into my everyday choices, and I gained the life skills which have put me where I am today.

I learned to be excellent in small, everyday things, like making sure my children understood their homework and keeping my house organized and clean in the midst of disappearing socks and other chaos. I challenged myself to grow and learn new things on my own. Balancing a home, family, kids' sports schedules, and a husband who traveled at the drop of a hat taught me time management and quick-adjustment skills.

When I finally established a career, my college journalism training helped me flush out motives from difficult clients during negotiations, write clear contracts, and communicate effectively with people from different socioeconomic and cultural backgrounds. Mastering these skills earned me the respect of brokers, bankers, attorneys, escrow agents, service center managers and other professionals, most of whom are men accustomed to dealing with other men.

Being an underdog in a rather cutthroat industry led to another necessary skill in planning for success. I learned how to say no.

"No" is an Important Vocabulary Word

Why does our society have an aversion to the word *no*? Some parenting books discourage its use. Psychology pundits advise redirection rather than refusal. But we lose something with all this so-called positive reinforcement. We lose the ability to tell others and even ourselves *no*.

Consider the relative ineffectiveness of the "Just say no to drugs" campaign. It wasn't a bad idea, but it was geared toward a nation with a disconnect from the word *no*. This is a systemic problem that perpetuates more negativity than positivity. We need to "just say no" to a lot more than drugs. Self-indulgence is crippling us.

Look at the increased consumer debt. Consider the number of unwanted pregnancies and extramarital affairs.

The US weight-loss market is worth $66 billion,[1] yet 70 percent of Americans are still overweight or obese.[2]

Many of us schedule every waking minute of every day with things that don't make a difference in the long run. Our inability to say no has us condensing space for our mental or spiritual development down to nothing. Or scheduling time with family and friends along with picking up the dry cleaning on our chore list. We fool ourselves into believing we are building strong relationships, yet our smartphones are always present at the dinner table, ready to whisk us away from intimate conversations.

If we want to stand out, we must learn how to use the word *no*. We must prioritize and establish boundaries. It's time to embrace the power in *not today* and *no thank you*. What we say no to defines our legacy every bit as much as what earns our *yes*.

I searched the internet for "how to say no" and came up with 1.4 billion results. It's a popular phrase. One of the top search results cited the late Steve Jobs, co-founder and long-serving chairman and CEO of Apple, who said, "People think focus means saying yes to the thing you've got to focus on. But that's not what it means at all. It means saying no to the hundred other good ideas. You have to pick carefully. I'm actually as proud of the things we haven't done as the things I have done. Innovation is saying no to 1,000 things."

If you want to be successful in the things that matter most, you must learn to say no to things that don't align with the legacy you are building. You may not have to cut things out completely, but learn how to limit them.

You don't have to serve on every committee.

Your kids don't need to play sports year-round.

You can deactivate your Facebook or Twitter account, even if just for a season.

You can turn down a dinner invitation with an acquaintance.

You can end a toxic relationship.

You can choose a more fulfilling job with less pay or fewer stressors.

You can fire demanding, unpleasant clients or employees.

You can set boundaries.

You can delegate or ask for help.

You can make little decisions every day to change your health.

When you say *no* to enough things that hold you back, you'll have more room to say *yes* to the activities that will transform your life.

When I decided I was going to write books, I embraced the philosophy "garbage in, garbage out" and quit watching R-rated movies. I may have missed out on a few good storylines, but overall, I didn't want what I shared to be distorted by constant exposure to the themes or scenes found in those movies. I needed my brain to be clear to write. That's a small example, but I'll be the first to admit not all sacrifices are easy.

One of the toughest things I've ever said no to is alcohol. I love a nice glass of Prosecco. There aren't very many varietals of red wine I don't know on a first-name basis. And I make a dang good margarita.

When you work in an industry where deals are done over cocktails, live in a country club neighborhood with a bar, and have friends who all drink, giving something up that you don't really have a problem with is painful. Yet I've walked away from that lifestyle for several years several times now, mostly when I'm writing.

If I want to lead people to blaze a path for others to follow, my speech can't be foggy or slurred. My mornings cannot be hazy. They are my most productive hours.

Sometimes we sacrifice for the greater good of others. Sometimes we sacrifice for our own good, even when we don't really like it. To do something great, we must plan for that success, not just act in the moment.

Strategize Decision-Making

According to various internet sources, people make somewhere between 27,000 and 35,000 choices a day. We have free will to make our own decisions about what to eat, wear, purchase, believe, pursue, or say. We choose who or what we will worship, whom we will marry, whom we will spend time with, etc. When we make decisions for employees or children, the number stretches toward the upper range.

In a 2015 article, Dr. Joel Hoomans, professor of management and leadership studies at Roberts Wesleyan College said each choice carries certain consequences— good and bad, and choices compound over time:

We see this most evidently in the choices we make with our spending and the way they collectively impact the balance sheet. These accumulated choices all work together over a lifetime to take us to various outcomes. Individual choices that concern only ourselves—such as what to eat for lunch—will seemingly only impact us personally, as they pertain to the time they require, the cost, the impact to our taste buds, energy level and health, etc. However, a leader's decisions always interact with others' choices and actions. These leadership decisions create a ripple effect for spouses, families, teams, business units, organizations, communities, states, nations and even the world-at-large.[3]

A 2015 Entrepreneur.com article highlights research related to the limits of our decision-making energies. "It turns out that the quality of our decisions begins to erode during the course of a typical day, as our fixed amount of willpower is used up. Stated differently, scientists have discovered that decision-making power is a *depletable resource*."[4]

This research has tremendous implications for managers at all types of companies. For the same reasons you are more likely to succumb to pizza and ice cream cravings at night after a day full of mentally-exhausting healthy decisions, you are more likely to make bad or hasty management decisions after a day full of hundreds of trivial judgments.

Reducing your non-critical decisions as much as possible frees your brain for more important high-order thinking. Many managers fail to realize that limiting decisions is not the same as limiting the expenditure of time or financial resources. It's easy to wonder, "Why should I fully delegate technical decisions to my CTO, or marketing decisions to my CMO, when it would take me ten minutes to review their proposals?"

The answer is that those ten minutes of actual "work" time might have cost you an hour's worth of your mental resources. The time it takes your brain to switch between various tasks can be tremendous when you're talking about high-level thinking. If time is money, then management's mental bandwidth is money squared.

Limiting your daily decisions does not only apply to delegating large management questions. It also applies to the little things throughout your day.

I do this by having routines. By planning some things in advance, I set myself up to stay on track better. I don't waste twenty minutes every morning trying to figure out what to wear. I compare the weather forecast and my calendar of events on Sunday and pull outfits for the entire week. When morning comes, I put on the next outfit, throw gym clothes in my bag, and I don't think about it again, unless I have to grab a sweater because the weatherman was wrong.

I do the same thing with my meals using a trick I learned from my sister-in-law Kendra. Her nutrition clients plan, shop for and prep an entire week's worth of meals on the weekend. Every morning they eat breakfast and place a lunch and one or two pre-measured snacks in a lunch bag, which helps keep them on track during the day. These types of routines can keep your progress from stalling on your most important goals. You set yourself up for success by planning ahead on the little things that otherwise suck up brain power or tempt you to deviate from what you know is best.

Always be Prepared

If people put as much effort into planning their life as planning a wedding, the world would be a vastly different place. We would be more focused on leaving a legacy than on having something old, something new, something borrowed, and something blue. Our days would be filled with purpose, each key part fitting into its proper place alongside the others. Our marriages, health, social lives, and hobbies would not be sacrificed to our financial woes, vocational pressures, or parenting issues. We could establish a healthy work-life balance.

Yes, I said work-life balance. I know a lot of people think that phrase is an oxymoron, or at least a completely unattainable ideal. That's a lie. When we know what's important, we can indeed have and do the things that matter most, thus defining our own work-life balance.

For me, that starts with an eternal perspective. I believe my life on earth is merely the preparation period before my reunion with God in heaven. Much like a wedding planner keeps all the details organized and moving in the right direction, I must keep the pieces of my life in order according to my purpose. We must come to terms with the fact we cannot be all things to all people, but I can be who I am supposed to be—and you can be who you are supposed to be. This aligns nicely with fulfilling our destiny. Each one of us has a unique contribution to make.

I wish I could say I was smart enough to figure this out on my own, but I am not. I'm more the type to put unnatural pressures on myself, wanting to "bring home the bacon, fry it up in the pan," like the 1980 perfume jingle suggests. We put a lot of pressure on ourselves to perform to the world's standards by being the best mom, daughter, co-worker, boss, volunteer, philanthropist, singer, teacher, or wife.

But at the end of our lives, the list goes no further than our epitaph. We don't happen upon a purpose-filled life. We must seek it. And then we must stay on it. This requires planning.

I draw a lot of comfort from the idea that all the planning for my life is not on my shoulders. God is the ultimate planner. From the beginning of time, when He created the Earth, He had a plan for humans' redemption. He told us about that plan throughout the Old Testament. There are more than three hundred prophecies in the Bible foretelling God's plan for the coming and life of Christ.

God didn't have a plan for just our redemption, He created a plan for each of our lives.

In Jeremiah 1:5, He says, "Before I shaped you in the womb, I knew all about you. Before you saw the light of day, I had holy plans for you." Later in the same book is a familiar passage to many of us. "For I know the plans I have for you," declares the Lord, "plans to prosper you and not to harm you, plans to give you hope and a future." In the Message translation, Jeremiah 29:11 reads like this, "I know what I'm doing. I have it all planned out—plans to take care of you, not abandon you, plans to give you the future you hope for."

In Proverbs 20:18, He exhorts us to "form your purpose by asking for counsel, then carry it out using all the help you can get."

It's much easier when we're young, isn't it? When we are in school, we show up at a scheduled time, attend lessons on specific subjects, learn certain things, study in whichever way is most effective for us, and pass tests to move on to the next level. We do get to make a few choices, but there's a clear framework.

This early education process serves a great purpose because it can show us where our passions and talents lie. School also teaches us how to schedule our lives around reaching certain goals. However, most of us lose some of the structure and discipline as we age. At least I did. For a long time, without the motivation of getting a silver dollar for every "A" on my report card, I lost appreciation for the careful planning required to achieve my goals.

In full disclosure, when I was in school, most of my planning centered around how little I could do to get what I wanted, but I'll attribute that to immaturity and an overzealous interest in boys. I've since learned if I apply myself, I can accomplish significant things in short periods of time. As a bonus, I often make progress on more than one thing at a time.

If we set goals and put a plan into motion for the full spectrum of our lives, we end up succeeding across the board. I have physical, financial, spiritual, marital, parental, vocational, emotional, intellectual, and social goals. These goals span hydration, retirement savings, reading my Bible in different versions, vacationing with my husband and grown children, growing professionally, journaling, reading business books, and developing meaningful relationships with other couples in the same stage of life.

I might have more focus on one than another on any given day, but I push forward on each area regularly. And I'm making progress toward a well-balanced life.

I mentioned earlier I didn't figure this out on my own. The person from whom I've learned the most about planning for success is businessman and leadership coach Michael Hyatt. I first began following Hyatt when he was the CEO of Thomas Nelson Publishing. Since then, I've tracked his success through his blog, a number of best-selling books, and most recently as my mentor.

In his book with Daniel Harkavy, *Living Forward*, Hyatt talks about having a life plan that's revisited every year. In his online curriculum and book, *Your Best Year Ever*, he breaks down planning by a year and or even a quarter at a time. This is where I began my journey of planning for success. I further grew in this capability by being able to make incremental progress toward my goals on a weekly and even daily basis. It's all about planning. And balance.

The first year I followed Hyatt's curriculum, I made great strides toward success. I graduated from college—twenty-five years after I dropped out to start a family. I wrote a book titled *Crushing Mediocrity* with my friend Lisa Copeland. I got my house in order by methodically cleaning every closet, every drawer, every cabinet, every nook and cranny to make sure things were organized. I emptied a two-hundred-square-foot storage unit and mostly purged my attic.

The following year, I took major steps toward budgeting and reducing debt. I know that may be shocking in my forties, but my excuse was that budgeting is challenging with a commission-based income. I got comfortable in front of a video camera and filmed an online course. I hired a writing coach to help me reshape a ten-year-old fiction writing project. I decided to pour more effort into mentoring younger women and found other like-minded women to join me in hosting a leadership forum. And for the first time since I started working full time, I sent out Christmas cards.

I've gone from feeling overwhelmed and aimless to feeling more organized, more rested, more fulfilled, and more ready for a new challenge. I hope I hang onto that discipline for the rest of my life. It's constant hard work, but the reward is worthwhile.

As a first-born, A-type personality, there's a story in the Bible that hits home for me. It tells of a man who went away on a trip and gave differing amounts of resources to several servants, depending on their abilities. When he returned, two of the servants had doubled what had been given them—investing the talents or treasures to present a profit. The third, and least capable, buried the treasure, using the excuse he didn't want to lose it.

Jesus said, "The master was furious. 'That's a terrible way to live! It's criminal to live cautiously like that! If you knew I was after the best, why did you do less than the least? The least you could have done would have been to invest the sum with the bankers, where at least I would have gotten a little interest'" (Matt. 25:14-30, MSG).

If you want a sure way to find success in life, the best thing to do is align yourself with God's will or purpose for your life and use your strengths, passions, and talents to create a return on the investment He made in you. Each one of us has been given special gifts, skills, and a time in history in which to use them. I discuss finding your specific purpose in more detail in a later chapter.

Eternally speaking, each one of us who claims Christ as Lord vies for the exact same success at the end of life— hearing the Father, on His judgement seat, uttering the words, "Well done, good and faithful servant."

Each year now, with purposeful planning and execution, I have more confidence. If I died today, I could give a good report about how I invested the talents and treasures God has given me.

If you need a starting place, I recommend reading *Your Best Year Ever*. But you can't just read it; you need to follow up, and you need accountability. I have found two groups of friends who hold me accountable. We check in with each other either weekly or quarterly, depending on the group. We encourage one another, celebrate our progress, revise our goals or reinvigorate progress toward achieving major milestones. Just knowing I have to report in helps me stay on track most of the time.

For those of you appreciate formulas, like me, Hyatt coaches you through believing in new possibilities, releasing the past, shaping your goals with motivation that will keep you going, and putting an action plan in place. I couple this with some task-management skills I learned in David Allen's *Getting Things Done: The Art of Stress-Free Productivity*. This is how I feed my need to check things off a list—and move my life toward a more meaningful end.

Life's curveballs remind me how important preparation is to success (and sanity). When I have a game plan, pivoting is easier, just like in sports.

Chapter 4

Fulfilling Your Destiny

I was the best bouncy-ball saleswoman in the state of Texas. Until I wasn't.

Roped into serving as the chairman of the PTA-run school store, I shopped and stocked and schemed to turn pencil vending into something interesting.

This is where the bouncy balls came in, along with middle-school locker mirrors and colorful erasers. But four weeks into the first semester, the principal decided little one-inch rubber balls were hazardous in classrooms of twelve-year-old boys. He shut down the sale of my highest profit item, and I had to adjust.

Yet, even in the face of this adversity, the store prospered, turning from a loss-leader for the PTA to a $12,000 profit-maker in year one. I recruited twenty student volunteers and more than forty parent volunteers over the school year. The following year I handed off what had become an iconic part of the Forbes Middle School experience to another sucker, er, volunteer, so I could take another role.

I face much higher stakes now. I've gone from being a PTA volunteer to selling private jets in some of the most elite circles in the world. A screw-up today could mean lives endangered or millions of dollars in liabilities. I deal with high-powered attorneys, bankers and billionaires, not freckled cheerleaders, brace-faced boys and drama-mamas.

I didn't not get to where I am overnight. I've learned each step of the journey builds upon the last. Fulfilling a destiny sometimes requires some trench trekking.

Don't Give Up

Early in 2008, without a clue about the impending recession, Curt and I decided to start an aircraft brokerage of our own. We had collaborated on projects before and found we worked well together. My organizational skills tempered his lofty ambitions. His tenacity overcame my risk aversion.

Our first client at Charlie Bravo Aviation was a large defense contractor. Our contact there suggested our company be certified as a woman-owned entity, because it could facilitate more contracts between our companies. We consulted our attorney, and Curt signed 1 percent of the company over to me. Instead of us being fifty-fifty partners, I was now the majority shareholder. We then applied to be certified and were rejected.

Turns out, the majority shareholder also must be the top officer, the highest compensated, and hold the most power and authority. We made those changes too. Being the head of a company full of arrogant salesmen in a male-dominated industry stretched me more than I ever could imagine.

After two years of reading books, attending leadership seminars, and being mentored, I still felt overwhelmed and under-respected in my role as CEO. People outside the company saw me as the company principal, but within the organization, I endured constant friction. And it wasn't just in the office. It spilled over into our home life as well.

I remember sitting in my home office in the Spring of 2011, crying out to God to get me out of this.

He led me to Genesis 37-41. I read the story of Joseph, who dreamed of a great destiny, which then seemed to be derailed by his jealous brothers. Sold into slavery, Joseph nonetheless rose to leadership in Potiphar's house before Potiphar's wife falsely accused him and had him thrown in jail.

Imprisoned again, Joseph served faithfully and rose to a leadership position. The warden put Joseph in charge of all those held in the prison, and he was made responsible for all that was done there. (See Genesis 39:22.)

As I meditated on the words in the Bible, it occurred to me that Joseph probably held the keys to the jail. He now possessed real-world leadership experience and marketable job skills. He held favor with the jailer, who probably wouldn't squawk too loud if he escaped.

The parallels did not escape my notice. I, too, had leadership experience, good connections, and marketable job skills. I, too, could choose a different path to success.

Joseph might have experienced success by taking the easy way out, but He would have missed his destiny—and changed the course of history.

The revelation helped me hang on through every discouraging day and difficult situation I've faced since then. Even when I felt like my circumstances were prison-like.

I know people who left situations that were abusive—to them or their kids—and I would not have counseled them otherwise. But other friends give up on unhappy marriages or trying careers—and live to regret it.

Don't Give Up on Others

One thing compounded my struggles with Charlie Bravo Aviation in the early years. My daughter. Brooke is one of those people who can light up a room with her smile and bright personality. On her cloudy days, however, everything in her vicinity reverberates with thunder. And Brooke's teenage years were stormy.

She'd be the first to tell you she made some bad decisions. She lost every shred of God-inspired peace she ever had and walked away from her faith, her family and any bright, hopeful future she may have envisioned for herself. Mired in misery, she lashed out at people and continued making choices that resulted in unhappiness.

If you also are a parent, you know the anguish her distress caused me. I wanted to absorb her heartache so she could return to the carefree, happy girl she once was. At times, her pain threatened to derail not only her purpose but mine as well.

I prayed nearly every day that God would take her to the end of herself and draw her back to His heart. That

He would restore her passion for life and others—and bring back my sunshine. She slowly emerged from the dark cloud, getting her esthetician license and moving to Colorado for a fresh start.

When things got rocky in the Colorado mountains, God brought her home through unusual circumstances. She hit a pothole while riding a type of skateboard and fractured her foot. She couldn't live in a third-floor apartment or support herself while recovering from the surgery she needed, so she moved back to Austin and back into our once-empty nest.

With a bone graft from her knee and eight titanium screws in her left foot, Brooke started over again, gradually making more and more healthy choices. As she grew stronger physically and spiritually, her relationship with me, Curt, and God improved. Curt's gift on her twenty-second birthday changed the trajectory of Brooke's life. She took a discovery flight in a four-seater Cessna 172, handling the controls and flying.

As I write this book, she is enrolled full time in flight school in Vero Beach, Florida, with her eyes on a commercial pilot's license. We are closer than ever now, so I know she's growing in her relationship with God. But I really knew she was in the center of God's will again when she called me, feeling guilty about enjoying her path so much. She's in school, studying and training more than sixty hours a week. It's the hardest she's worked in her life. Yet she wondered if she was neglecting what God wanted her to be doing because she didn't feel like she was sacrificing enough.

I chuckled at her joy. When we align ourselves with God, even if we face adversity, we win. I reminded Brooke that in Psalm 37:4, we are told if we delight ourselves in the Lord, He will give us the desires of our heart. He wants us to be delighted. And when we find that delight in Him, He can set the jet streams to give us an updraft at the right time to propel us in the right direction and make our hearts soar.

Sometimes you must persevere. Other times, fulfilling your destiny requires change.

The Power of Disruption

My great-grandparents drove some of the first gasoline-powered automobiles. They were among the first women to vote in the United States. They were the first generation with telephones, electricity, radios, televisions, dishwashers, and vacuum cleaners in their homes. They were alive during the first powered flight and the first man on the moon—and all this innovation happened despite the disruption of two world wars and the Great Depression.

I came of age as the internet first emerged. My generation was the first to use cordless phones, car phones, brick phones, cell phones, iPhones, and whatever else has come out by the time this book lands in your hands.

I believe God placed us in this generation uniquely equipped to face our own set of challenges and interruptions—no matter how fast they come at us.

An article by Greg Satell, originally published on Digital Tonto, said of the next decade:

> While the digital laws may seem to be working steadily on our behalf, the numbers can be deceiving because they actually represent accelerating returns... We will advance roughly the same amount in the next eighteen months as we did in the previous thirty years. Whereas previous tech waves transformed business and communication, the next phase will be marked by technology so pervasive and important, we'll scarcely know it's there.[1]

In aviation, we are watching the development of passenger drones, self-flying vehicles that will radically change how we manage airspace and travel. Innovative retail companies are anticipating great changes as well, one of which will be virtual sales people at kiosks powered by artificial intelligence. We call these major advances disrupters.

Disrupters can be good.

I love the storyline of the movie *Hidden Figures*. One of the central characters, Dorothy Vaughan, served as the acting supervisor for the Colored female mathematicians. In 1961, she saw a threat to her livelihood in the new IBM computer at NASA. Instead of bemoaning the demise of her job, she studied computer programming on her own and tackled the beast. Dorothy's foresight created an opportunity to be promoted, not only for her, but for her entire team of women at NASA.

Disrupters also can be bad.

Families are disrupted by divorce. Lives are hijacked by terrorism or disease. Cars crash. Pets die. People make mistakes. You must decide how you're going to handle the disruptions in your life or sphere of influence.

You may need to change a lifestyle, a career, or a direction when a disrupter materializes. Be open to new ideas and know each one may require a different approach. Dig deep and find the courage to stand up.

Don't Let Your Past Rob Your Future

Many of us have a checkered past, and some have more checkers than others. Bad choices have a knack for following us, even after we've turned things around and become successful. This happened to my friend Rebecca Contreras.

Rebecca was born to a poverty-stricken, drug-addicted Hispanic mother in the late 1960s. She's one of four children, none of whom knew their fathers. As a child, Rebecca grew up in poverty, neglected and abused, a product of the trials that often plague children of single parents ill-equipped to provide for them.

Rebecca dropped out of high school and began working as a cocktail waitress at age seventeen. An unexpected pregnancy complicated matters. So, in the delivery room, she passed her daughter Crystaline to her (now drug-free) mom.

After a year of drinking, drugs, and irresponsible living, Rebecca gave in to her mom's pleas to attend church.

During an evening tent revival, Rebecca experienced a life-changing encounter with God, flushed her drugs down the toilet, and made a firm commitment to get her life on track. At the age of nineteen, Rebecca began the journey that turned around her life.

She took responsibility for Crystaline, got her GED, enrolled in the Texas Welfare-to-Work Program, and met a dynamic youth pastor to whom she has now been married for twenty-eight years. Rebecca was promoted at several state personnel agencies by learning how to maneuver office politics and increasing job responsibilities with finesse. Her tenacity earned her a position working for then-Governor George W. Bush.

Bec, as he calls her, still worked for him when he was elected president. As a star employee, Rebecca faced a major choice: keep her family in Texas with the jobs they knew or move to Washington, D.C. to start over.

After much deliberation and prayer, Rebecca and her husband David sold their house and moved their family across the country to join President Bush. She was commissioned as a member of his White House staff in the position of special assistant to the president and associate director of presidential personnel. In this role, she oversaw the president's appointments to more than 1,200 part-time board and commission positions within the federal government.

Part of the onboarding process for this federal job was a detailed background investigation. The Secret Service uncovered unsavory things in Rebecca's past—

information that could cause the administration angst. The past Rebecca thought she'd left far behind caught up with her and knocked her out at the knees.

With her heart in her stomach, she headed into the West Wing office of the presidential personnel director. Before this, Rebecca had been private about her past, not wanting her teenage history to cost her future opportunities. The choices before her were to deny the findings, downplay or discredit them, or to admit her mistakes and be held accountable for her actions.

She decided to tell her boss the whole sordid story. Because of Rebecca's transparency and the trust she had earned, the director went to bat for her. The job was not compromised. If anything, she garnered more respect as a woman who had faced tremendous odds as a child, overcame them, and moved forward as an adult.

Rebecca is a great example of someone who took responsibility for her past and her choices without letting them define her as a person.

After completing her White House post, Rebecca was appointed to serve on the board of the West Point Military Academy and at the Department of US Treasury in the role of deputy assistant secretary and chief human capital officer. Her duties included overseeing corporate human resources for a workforce of approximately 128,000 employees.

Today she runs her own company and is *crushing it* as a federal contractor with expertise in organizational development, human capital, and technology. She serves on the board of the American Bible Society as chair of the

movement he helped spawn continue to shape the 21st."
Best-selling author and *CT* Editor-at-Large Philip Yancey's
tribute article summarized some highlights:

> We can measure the greatness of the man by
> noting his impression on a movement that
> emerged from fundamentalist roots. Billy
> Graham did not invent the word *evangelical*,
> but he managed to restore the word's original
> meaning—"good news"—both for the skeptical
> world and for the beleaguered minority who
> looked to him for inspiration and leadership.
>
> …when he stepped behind a pulpit, whether
> speaking to a small group at the White House or
> the Kremlin, or to millions gathered outdoors
> in Korea or in Central Park, something
> supernatural happened. All other concerns of
> life faded away, and he focused like a laser
> beam on the one sure thing he knew: the gospel
> of Jesus Christ and its power to change lives.[2]

Can you imagine his reception in heaven? I bet the
receiving line was a billion people long.

As we explore our specific purpose on earth and look
to leave our own legacy, the question we must ask is when
we depart this earth is: will we have done everything we
could to fulfill our destiny?

This question in my life resulted in me writing this
book. When I look at the difficulty of selling airplanes and
the frustrations of my oft-stressful job, I sometimes think
that's enough. I tithe, I pay taxes, and I mentor others.

But then I talk to women who think I'm a role model, who are somehow inspired by me, who have drawn strength from a story I've told, and I know that selling multi-million dollar jets is selling myself short. I have an obligation to help others rise to their feet, overcome their obstacles, and take a bow at their own standing ovation.

That's my legacy. Helping others stand up is your destiny too. You may fail a few times along the way, but those setbacks enrich our story, improve our empathy, and make good fodder from which others can learn.

Chapter 5

Recovering from Failure

S everal years after Curt and I started Charlie Bravo Aviation, I decided to start a sister company named Charlie Bravo Charter. I assembled a team, created a brand, and began selling private charter flights. My advertisements caught the eye of Circuit of the Americas (COTA), a new company in Austin with big-name investors and a lot of international media attention.

Most international tourists thought of Houston or Dallas when Texas came up in conversation, but COTA was putting Austin on the map. The organization was bringing Formula One back to the United States after a long hiatus by building a racetrack on the outskirts of Austin to host the US Grand Prix. I saw a potential partnership with COTA as a feather in my cap, a way to gain media attention and secure a good reputation among charter operators and clients alike.

The contract negotiations took nearly six months. But in July 2012, Charlie Bravo Charter was finally named the official charter partner of the first Grand Prix in Austin, with the race scheduled four months later. The company would provide charter on fixed wing aircraft into and out of Austin, as well as helicopter shuttles between downtown and the racetrack.

My team secured helicopters, pilots and an experienced operations team to make sure things ran smoothly during the three-day race event, which required us to have eighteen different helicopters in operation. I learned more than I ever imagined there was to know about helicopters, including how much room they need to take off and what helicopter pilots consider as dangerous operational conditions.

I had a crash course in helipad approval and helicopter operations over commercial airports because the Austin-Bergstrom International Airport was situated directly between downtown and the track—five nautical miles from the city and just two from the racetrack. I worked with the air traffic controllers at the Austin airport to make sure there would be no interference with scheduled airline flights. I coordinated with the FAA to expedite the approval of two new helipads in the Austin area.

I navigated the politics of neighborhood associations that didn't want helicopter noise and FAA departments that didn't want to allow hot refueling, a practice which allows helicopters to be refueled with the rotors spinning.

Contractually promised first right of refusal on all the landing slots at the racetrack's six helipads, Charlie Bravo Charter began taking reservations from VIPs and dignitaries from all over the world.

I met with Steve Henry of Henry Aviation, who agreed to mentor me. His company had been hired to oversee the helipad construction at the track and to direct helicopter landings on the days of the event. Steve had been coordinating helicopter traffic for years at races. Three months before the race, he stopped to help a stranded motorist and was smashed by an oncoming car. He spent six weeks fighting for his life in intensive care before starting rehab. The race weekend was his first outing. It was a miracle he could work at all, let alone help me with my organization.

In the week before the race, we were beset by several additional catastrophes.

The operations company I'd hired several months before to dispatch helicopters on race days backed out with no notice and no reason. In desperation, I called the assistant chief helicopter pilot for the state of Texas. He rounded up some officers who could help with walkie-talkies and keep their cool in chaotic surroundings. A helicopter pilot recently retired from the US Army volunteered to take over operations for the busiest helipad.

If I wasn't under enough pressure a few days before the race, the City of Austin decided no helicopter operations could take place after dark in the city, even with proper lighting. With the race ending at 4:30 in the afternoon a month before the shortest day of the year, I decided to redirect all the downtown passengers to the Austin airport and provide limos to take them back to the city instead of having them land where they took off. Not only was this decision unpopular with VIPs, it also threw Governor Perry's security detail into a frenzy, as they would have to make a significant number of changes to their security plan.

To compound matters, the day before the race, the FAA and air traffic controllers decided all helicopter traffic needed to be rerouted ten miles south of the airport. This meant that a five-minute flight from downtown to the track would now take twenty minutes each way.

Traffic was significantly less congested on Friday and Saturday than on Sunday, but when Sunday rolled around, we were already tired. For whatever reason, Steve Henry's company did not give our helicopters first right of refusal to land and take off from the track. Circling helicopters were in a holding pattern for as long as forty-five minutes, requiring several of them to return to the airport to refuel instead of picking up passengers.

Pilots were irritable, and passengers, who had been warned there would be somewhat of a wait, were furious. COTA employees were completely unavailable to help. After the race, they avoided my calls for nearly two months, forcing me to refund some clients' fares on my own, even though COTA had failed to live up to the terms of the contract requiring it to provide all the priority landings to Charlie Bravo Charter.

I counted it as a success that we completed 2,100 operations in three days without a single incident, not even a sprained ankle on the uneven ground where the helicopters landed at the track. But the overall customer experience was far below what I had hoped to provide.

It devastated me. After the race was over, I tucked my tail like a kicked dog and hid in my dark bedroom. For three days. I can't remember if I ate. I'm pretty sure I didn't change out of pajamas. I know I didn't check my email. I had nothing left to give.

After licking my wounds for several months, I realized that sometimes you accomplish what seemed impossible and still, for reasons outside of your control, you fail. Even though we were flexible and responsive in meeting each challenge, Charlie Bravo Charter's reputation and profitability suffered.

Instead of looking back on the experience as time poorly spent, I choose to remember I made good connections, kept people safe, and learned a lot about charter operations and helicopters. I certainly now know to ask more questions about how partners will perform their expected tasks. And today, I use that experience in analyzing clients' private aircraft missions from both a financial and a complexity standpoint.

Some failure may be inevitable, but there is always a silver lining in the cloud of dust stirred up by a big fleet of helicopters or any other obstacle. You may have to wait for it to settle to see the positive. Things that seem like failures today can be the launching pad for incredible turnarounds and spectacular finishes in the future. To achieve success from failure, we must learn from it and use it to accelerate ourselves toward a different place. Otherwise, we end up in a repetitive cycle of failing again, stuck perpetually in mediocrity—or worse.

Perhaps the types of failures that hurt most are the ones where we knew better and still made the stupid mistake—often for instant gratification—that affected our family, our workplace, or our community. Extramarital affairs, accidents caused by texting while driving, and living beyond our means all have devastating ripple effects.

Even when we make things right, forgiving ourselves for making the mistake in the first place can be difficult and often cripples us from making healthy decisions in the future. Guilt can freeze us in the worst places. This is when failure morphs from the professor who can teach us a lesson to the warden that imprisons us. We must make a conscious decision to go on while also putting safeguards in place to avoid failure again.

Accept that Failure is Part of Success

I grew up listening to Paul Harvey's famous broadcasts themed *The Rest of the Story*. For more than four decades, Harvey began his stories with little-known facts on a variety of subjects omitting a key element until the end, when he revealed the rest of the story, usually the name of a well-known person or event. His presentations served as a constant reminder that success can (and usually does) come after facing a major obstacle or failure.

Life is not a game where some are winners and some are losers. We all experience failure. However, God has given each one of us the opportunity for an ultimate victory. Our biggest responsibility is to stand back up.

Because often, what we perceive as failure is a means to a more profound triumph.

If we are to rise from mediocrity, we cannot allow failures or setbacks to hold us back for the rest of our lives. The loss of a relationship, an unprofitable year, or a failed business may determine the turn in the path we take, but we must rise above our circumstances. According to several sources, eight out of ten entrepreneurs who start a business will fail at some point. Regardlesss of whether that statistic is accurate or skewed, if everyone who failed the first time gave up, the world would be a far more primitive place.

We can learn a lot from some of the world's most persistent people.

Walt Disney was fired from the *Kansas City Star* newspaper because his editor felt he "lacked imagination and had no good ideas."[1] He lost several businesses in the animation field due to lack of money, he was swindled by a distributor, and then he had trouble selling his early Mickey Mouse animations. Without Walt Disney's determination, our childhoods would have been significantly different.

Colonel Sanders of Kentucky Fried Chicken fame lost several jobs and his law practice by brawling with colleagues. He was well-versed in changing jobs. By the time he was thirty, he'd worked as a farmer, painter, teamster, blacksmith's helper, railway custodian, fireman, train conductor, lawyer, life insurance salesman, and ferryboat company owner. It wasn't until he was in his sixties that Sanders franchised the concept of his special-recipe fried chicken and found his success. Even in retirement, he kept pushing.

Oprah Winfrey, the richest African American of the twentieth century, was not raised with a silver spoon in her mouth. Despite a troubled childhood, by nineteen, she was the first African-American woman to anchor the news in Nashville. Her position didn't last though. She was fired because of her sincere compassion; her voice trembled when she reported a decrease in stock rates or another hurricane devastating a coastline. Eventually, she was invited to host a low-rated half-hour morning talk show in Chicago. Her determination not to change her heartfelt style revolutionized the media industry.

Thomas Edison is possibly the most illustrious example of failure—and success—in modern history.

Amid thousands of failures, Edison's inventions that did succeed launched new industries. Without electric light, utility power distribution, sound recording, and motion pictures, Oprah Winfrey, Walt Disney, and Colonel Sanders would not have built the empires they did.

"Our greatest weakness lies in giving up," Edison said. "The most certain way to succeed is always to try just one more time."

Failure can be a stepping stone if you use it in the right way.

Failure is a necessary part of success. It helps you remain humble. It promotes growth. You must not be afraid to look foolish or lose face. You must know when not to take failure personally. Like Edison, you must commit to success despite setbacks. And you must know the worst is usually not as bad as you imagined it could be.

In the late 1990s, one of the most anticipated new baseball players was a man who knew tremendous success in life and athletics: Michael Jordan. The three-time champion and sports icon left the NBA to pursue his love of baseball and a the chance to be a star in another sport. The harsh reality was that this mega-star went to a minor league baseball team, rode on buses not nearly as comfortable as the cars he owned, and took a beating from reporters and spectators all over the country. While he was the best basketball player of his time, his talents in baseball proved subpar. He played for two minor league teams in his attempt to get the call to the big leagues, but it never came.

Jordan was asked over and over, "What made you keep trying baseball after you failed?" When he returned to the NBA, two years after leaving, Nike came out with a commercial that summed up his thoughts on what makes a winner: He said, "I've missed more than 9,000 shots in my career. I've lost almost 300 games. Twenty-six times I've been trusted to take the game-winning shot and missed. I've failed over and over and over again in my life…and that is why I succeed."

Sometimes We Must Blaze a Path

As a society, we are handicapping the generation behind ours, the generation that overwhelmingly wants to be difference makers and world changers. We have celebrated "good enough" and "great try" and offered reassurances like "we're not going to let you fail" and "no child gets left behind." We have made inclusion a greater priority than excellence. The problem is that we are not teaching fortitude, drive, tenacity, or perseverance.

Maybe we should let those younger than us fail, so they learn how to pick themselves up, brush themselves off, and run to catch up. That's how confidence is built. If we don't teach them how to crush mediocrity after failure and stand a head above the crowd, we may rob them of the future they otherwise could live. And the compounding effect as generations come and go will be disastrous.

The most effective way to teach our children to succeed after failure is to do it ourselves—and as much as is appropriate for their age, let them see the struggle that it takes for us to do it. My neighbor Joe tries all sorts of crazy things when it comes to building strength and stamina. I've seen him out running wind sprints with a mask that simulates high altitude. He jogs in the heat of one-hundred-degree summer days with a sweat suit on. And recently, he took his golf cart to the bottom of the hill with a sled and his fifty-pound free weights so he could pull them uphill strapped around his waist.

The next weekend, I saw his teenaged daughter with the same setup, pulling an empty sled then gradually adding more weights. I'm not sure what sport she plays or what setbacks she's experienced, but her willingness to prepare for a harder path will take her a long way.

We never know who is watching us press forward.

Several of my friends have divorced after twenty or more years of marriage. The emotions they experience are heart wrenching, especially if they've been abandoned for a younger woman after spending two decades raising children. The betrayal, loneliness and fear of the future can choke any hope for a bright outlook.

As women, we are wise to develop marketable job skills while staying at home with our children, if we are blessed to do that. Having a way to make a living after any sort of life change benefits both us and our families—even if it does no more than provide a sense of satisfaction and purpose once we become empty nesters.

If you find yourself in this position, I'd counsel you, as I have others, to remember why you are here. Be grateful for the things that have not failed. Put together two or three clear, measurable goals on which you can focus and succeed. Surround yourself with good people. You can recover.

If you are not in a time of change, you would be smart to prepare as if you were. Because it will come. And how you handle it will mean the difference between failure and opportunity for something new.

We Fail. God Doesn't.

I've talked a lot about the challenges I've faced—an unexpected pregnancy, abandoning college plans, getting married, becoming a company leader, losing at business, managing an empty nest, and doubting myself. Through it all, I've found that if I lift my eyes up, my perspective shifts. When I place my hope in the Lord, I find an anchor in the storm. I don't lose who I am. No matter how fierce my trials, tempests or temptations, God can and will pull good from it. He will do it for you too.

Probably the best-known example of this is in Jesus' crucifixion. Put yourself in the disciples' sandals for a moment. They left their jobs and families to follow the deliverer of Israel, only to watch him die a miserable death. How could they have been so off target? Don't we sometimes question ourselves in the same way? But like God, who brought Jesus back from the dead, we can gain glory from our pain as well.

Whether you believe in the Bible or not, it's undeniable that Christianity has successfully spread and grown throughout the last 2,000 years. With an estimated 2.2 billion followers, Christianity is the largest organization in the world.[2] However, its unlikely start with a group of twelve commoners and a thirty-year-old wanderer seemed doomed to failure when its leader died a criminal's death and his followers scattered in fear. Every analyst in the world would bet against the likelihood of success coming from that scenario.

Even after Jesus rose from the dead and the church was born, constant persecution forced these Christians and their converts to move from their lands. But instead of destroying the movement, this persecution forced the gospel's dissemination throughout civilization. Clearly, before we consider something to be a failure, we need to know the rest of the story. What may appear to be a failure from one viewpoint could be seen as the beginning of success from another perspective.

Failure is not optional. We all fail. Opting not to learn from it is another story. You cannot be successful if you aren't prepared to take risks, and an inherent part of risk is, of course, failing. Use your own strength and the strength God has given you to stand up again after you fall. Your scars serve less as a reminder of when you went down, and more as proof that you got up and kept going.

Chapter 6

Restoring Harmony

One of the biggest contributors to unprecedented levels of hate and ugliness in our communities is a lack of consequences. Being spiteful or unkind is easy when the offender never needs to face the person they've reviled. But I imagine this kind of behavior would decrease if those who were dishing it out were forced to face the person they bullied.

I still remember the humiliation of having an eighth-grade teacher intercept a note I wrote to a friend that contained some gossip about a classmate. To my embarrassment, the teacher read the note out loud to the class. I had to look that poor, maligned classmate in the face in the lunch line, mortified by being caught. She laughed it off when I apologized, but the humiliation sticks with me even now.

To restore the harmony our social media practices have all but destroyed, we must build community by both having friends and being a friend to others:

...In Our Families

My closest friend is my sister Amy. We talk on the phone nearly every day. We've coached each other through ups and downs, teenaged kids, family frustrations, career and financial challenges and more. We occasionally get mad at each other—not like when we were kids and I pushed her down the stairs for taking my lipstick, but still upset. As adults, we've learned the value of our relationship is worth setting aside our differences.

I've also formed deep relationships with Curt's extended family. Thirty (and growing) of us get together in a big house at the beach at least every other year. There's tension sometimes, especially with a lot of big personalities all in one house. The beach volleyball games do get a little aggressive. But we love and cherish each other, despite our differences. Of the four core families who started the tradition, all of us came from divorced parents, yet none of us have ever gone there. Combined, we represent more than 100 years of marriage.

Our kids are all close, even though they span twenty years in ages, and they live in four different states. They check in with each other weekly, cheer for one another, and hold each other accountable. They are all friends. That doesn't happen by accident.

...In Our Neighborhoods

Remember block parties? Progressive dinners? When's the last time you attended one? Do you know your neighbors' names? When we moved into our first house in

Texas, we were on a loop of about forty homes. I took the initiative to get everyone together for an annual barbeque. Several of the guys started smoking meat at five o'clock in the morning. Beers were chilled by noon. We blocked off the road with cars (which was probably illegal). And kids ran around with water balloons and squirt guns.

As a result of our efforts to foster relationships among our community, we knew when Nancy got cancer. We rallied around Robin when Tim died. We celebrated basketball and football victories together. Sarazen Loop became the most sought-after street in the subdivision. When someone had to move, their house was barely on the market before it was under contract. We built community. We were neighbors in the truest sense of the word. All it took was setting a date for a block party.

...In Our Churches

If overall church attendance is anemic, church involvement might be a mere blink from extinction in many congregations. When I was a child, my parents always went to couples' Sunday School. When a family moved, the Sunday School class helped. When a baby was born or someone was sick, meals appeared right on schedule. The leaders met with members of the class who were struggling. Lifelong friendships were born.

Modern churches, like the one I attend, often don't have capacity for everyone to be on campus at the same time on Sunday mornings. They compensate with small groups for this type of intimate interaction. These community-based groups provide a powerful connection. Find one. Heck, start one.

...In Our Community

Curt and I have a group of friends we hang out with regularly. Typically we go to dinner at each other's houses or a restaurant. At one particular birthday party, we decided to mix it up the following year, doing something different each month: hiking, boating, attending a rodeo, going to a basketball game, serving in a soup kitchen, playing putt-putt. I even consented to zip lining, which is way outside my comfort zone. All for the sake of strengthening our friendships. It works.

My son Jake embraced community in a non-traditional form in college. As a part of his campus church, he got involved in Fort Worth's homeless community. From the "bagels and bingo" outreach, Jake formed a homeless basketball team and enrolled it in the recreation center's basketball league. They lost every game. But they had a blast. They built community. And they raised awareness of the homeless plight in Fort Worth by interacting with men from other teams.

...In Our Workplaces

Two primary things make me feel isolated in my work. Leaders often feel alone in their roles, especially when things are not going well or they've made a tough decision. I have often felt isolated or left out as a woman in a man's world. After fifteen years, there are still a couple of old timers who don't acknowledge me at conferences.

It wasn't until I joined an organization called the International Aviation Women's Association (IAWA) and got involved on the board that I realized trying to fit in with the guys was the wrong approach. I found myself more fulfilled in my career and more equipped in my job when I built a community of like-minded and similarly challenged individuals.

Now industry events feel like family reunions. There's a powerful network of industry leaders engaged, and there's common ground to forge new relationships with women from Australia, South Africa, Afghanistan, Austria and Aruba, to name the ones that start with A. My industry community is powerful, connected, and willing to help with just about anything. Best of all, I belong there.

Gallup observed that employees who reported having a best friend at work were:

- 43 percent more likely to report having received praise or recognition for their work in the last seven days.
- 37 percent more likely to report that someone at work encourages their development.
- 35 percent more likely to report coworker commitment to quality.
- 28 percent more likely to report that in the last six months, someone at work has talked to them about their progress.

- 27 percent more likely to report that the mission of their company makes them feel their job is important.
- 27 percent more likely to report that their opinions seem to count at work.
- 21 percent more likely to report that at work, they have the opportunity to do what they do best every day. [7]

The best managers in the world observe that the quality and depth of employees' relationships is a critical component of employee loyalty. This item also points to the issue of trust between coworkers. When strong engagement is felt in a workgroup, employees believe their coworkers will help them during times of stress and challenge. In this day of rapid-fire change, reorganization, mergers, and acquisitions, having best friends at work may be the true key to effective change integration and adaptation. When compared to their peers, employees who have best friends at work identify significantly higher levels of healthy stress management, even though they experience the same levels of stress.

...In Our Sphere of Influence

Former US Surgeon General Vivek Murthy, who served from 2014 to 2017, said his staff grew quickly as presidential appointments were made and staffers were hired. "Although team members got along well, it soon became clear that we didn't fully recognize the rich life experience that each person brought to the team," he said. "We had a decorated Army nurse, a woman who had spent years providing medical care to prison inmates, an accomplished pianist and preacher, an Olympic-level runner, and several team members who had struggled with addiction in their family. Even though we were operating with the formality and hierarchy of a uniformed service, my team was hungry to know more about each other."[2]

To build community, they developed "Inside Scoop," an exercise in which team members were asked to share something about themselves through pictures for five minutes during weekly staff meetings:

> The impact was immediate. These sessions quickly became many people's favorite time of the week, and they were more enthusiastic about participating at staff meetings. People felt more valued by the team after seeing their colleagues' genuine reactions to their stories. Team members who had traditionally been quiet during discussions began speaking up. Many began taking on tasks outside their traditional roles. They appeared less stressed at work. And most of them told me how much more connected they felt to their colleagues and the mission they served.

We Must Be Vulnerable

Isn't it strange how we can feel both more connected and less connected at the same time? We're connected in more ways with more people through social media, email, group texting, and video interactions on services like

Skype or FaceTime. We're less connected because those interactions are typically brief or superficial.

Deep, life-long relationships, where conflict arises and problems are overcome, have dwindled. Divorce rates continue to rise in the United States. And many Europeans don't even bother to get married.

It takes hard work to stay married, let alone to feel connected and close in our marital partnerships. We must have the hard conversations in a grownup manner, even if it feels like exposing a tender jugular.

Painful as it may seem, vulnerability in marriage makes a huge difference. And when your life partner doubles as your business partner, vulnerabilities multiply. Not too long ago, I was doubting a business decision I made, feeling insecure about a personal goal, and stressed about some financial things. When I finally sat down and told Curt my feelings and frustrations, he shared some of his with me. As simple as the gesture was, it reignited our marriage and drew us closer together. When our personal relationship is strong, our business benefits from the unity. Vulnerability can help. However, this exposure also creates a risk that can hurt us.

Jeff Booth, co-founder and CEO of BuildDirect, says CEOs experience loneliness because of fear and/or ego:

> On the one hand, there's fear of appearing inadequate and that asking for help could make others doubt your judgement. Meanwhile, your ego tells you that you really don't need others to help make big decisions—who

knows your business better than you do? Combined, these two factors can prevent even highly capable CEOs from turning to others for much needed support.

Vulnerability is all about inviting others into your world (however messy), which makes it a natural antidote to loneliness. The challenge is taking that first step and letting down your defenses. I've found that simply trusting first and asking questions later can dramatically accelerate ties with your team.[3]

When you cannot involve a member of your team, a mentor or peer group like Vistage or Young President's Organization (YPO) helps. Even the Bible echoes the need for input.

Proverbs 15:22 suggests, "Plans fail for lack of counsel, but with many advisers they succeed." More than once, this verse and principle encouraged me to ask for help. Especially if you are a role model, other people appreciate when you show you aren't unflappable. It improves authenticity and allows others to know the real you.

We Need Alone Time

I need time to myself. Just typing it makes me want to jump up and shout the word "need." I don't know what I'd do if Curt didn't golf every weekend. When it rains for days on end, I sometimes ask him to go to the golf club and hang out there so I can have the house to myself. I get up earlier in the morning than he does so

I can have time to myself before he stumbles into the kitchen for coffee.

This time to journal, pray, think, fold laundry, unload the dishwasher, or stare at the fireplace defines my days and weeks. To retain my sanity, I have to guard my quiet time. It calibrates me.

In his book *Soul Keeping*, John Ortberg examines what it means to have a healthy soul that's connected to God and others in a culture starved by busyness and the pursuit of status and wealth. The self, Ortberg claims, is way too small a unit to be able to bear the weight of a life alone.

Ortberg believes one of the most effective cures for the drain that comes from a hurried, frantic pace in this technological age is to set aside regular periods of time to spend in solitude. It's an idea which, at first blush, people struggling with loneliness might fear will exacerbate their feeling of isolation:

Ironically, one of the things you discover in solitude is that you're not alone. A big difference between Jesus and most folks in our day is Jesus was often alone but never lonely. We are often lonely but hardly ever truly alone...

> A lot of people wonder what they're supposed to do in a period of solitude. The main point isn't what to do, but what not to do. We don't hurry or try to produce. Our bodies and minds realize we still have worth as human beings when we're not doing anything, and we realize that God and the world get along okay without our striving. We begin to realize how much of our

'to-do' list is about our ego more than anything else. Eventually, our souls begin to rest, and we discover we'd rather live this way. Instead of obligation, solitude becomes a lifeline.[4]

Spending time with God and getting refilled enables us to give to others without feeling drained. Whether you are the CEO of a company, the pastor of a church, the president of a country, or a single parent with kids at home, the pressures and decisions you face are weighty and constant. This is why God gives us so many leadership examples in the Bible. From Moses to Daniel, Jesus to Paul, there are principles to affirm, words to comfort, and commands to encourage and direct us. I honestly don't know how leaders who don't follow Christ handle their stress. I couldn't survive.

While there is much strength in fellowship with others, especially other believers within a church community, loneliness might be a gift from the Lord, designed to draw us closer to Him.

Psalm 34:17-18 tells us, "The Lord hears his people when they call to him for help. He rescues them from all their troubles. The Lord is close to the brokenhearted; he rescues those whose spirits are crushed." (NLT) Proverbs 18:24 assures us, "One who has unreliable friends soon comes to ruin, but there is a friend who sticks closer than a brother."

When there is no one else with whom we can possibly find to commiserate, and we can't depend on ourselves, we turn to Him. His greatest desire lies in relationships with the humans He created. Intimacy with God is where we find our best inspiration and comfort. Here God can gently correct us when we are off course in our leadership or life, instead of waiting until we turn back to Him in a time of disaster.

We Need to Help Others

I have found my loneliest moments exacerbated by self-focus. When I turn from self-pity to selflessness, the loneliness dissipates. Serving others seems to defuel depression and apathy. Lending an ear to someone whose husband is cheating makes me forget my irritation that Curt rarely does the dishes. Helping someone figure out where they will live after eight feet of water flooded their house makes a delay in repairing my air conditioner seem insignificant.

When I reach out to others, I find my gratitude for what I have swelling. It displaces my dissatisfaction and depression.

If finding your way out of a pit of despair isn't motivating enough, consider the far-reaching implications of your involvement in society, in your family, your neighborhood, your church, your community, your workplace, your personal or professional sphere of influence. What if you start with those who will most influence your future—today's children—and those who have most impacted your present—today's elderly?

According to Victoria Prooday, occupational therapist and writer at YourOT.com, "There is a silent tragedy developing right now, in our homes, and it concerns our most precious jewels—our children... Researchers have been releasing alarming statistics on a sharp and steady increase in kids' mental illness, which is now reaching epidemic proportions:

- 1 in 5 children has mental health problems
- 43 percent increase in ADHD
- 37 percent increase in teen depression
- 200 percent increase in suicide rate in kids 10-14 years old"[5]

According to an article on *TIME.com*, "Despite the rise in teen depression, the study, which analyzed data from the National Surveys on Drug Use and Health, reported that there wasn't a corresponding increase in mental health treatment for adolescents and young adults. Researchers said this is an indication that there is a growing number of young people who are under-treated or not treated at all for their symptoms."[6]

The article goes on to say it's not just teenagers, it's young kids—in elementary school:

> Counselors like Ellen Chance in Palm Beach say they see evidence that technology and online bullying are affecting kids' mental health as young as fifth grade, particularly girls. I couldn't tell you how many students are being malicious to each other over Instagram. I've had cases where girls don't to come to school, and they are cutting themselves and becoming severely depressed because they feel outcasted and targeted.

Chance says she now sees cutting incidents weekly at her elementary school, and while they vary in severity, it's a signal that not all is right.

We desperately need to stand up and do something. If you are a parent, be a parent.

Put down *your* phone.

Talk to your kids.

Play games.

Have a picnic.

Schedule adventures.

Create memories.

Build a tree house. Together *with* them. Not *for* them.

The best legacy you can offer your kids is a sense of belonging.

People need people. I love the story of a United Kingdom initiative that pairs young professionals who need to live in the city for work with elderly people who own a city dwelling and need companionship.

Ranjana Srivastava, an Australian oncologist and author spent more than two decades making rounds in the hospitals she served, observing the toll of isolation upon the elderly and infirm:

> Few things console the elderly and give them more purpose than knowing that they matter to someone. It's moving to see how pain dissipates and anxiety fades in the presence of loved ones. But when you look down the vacant corridors of the hospital or tally vain attempts to engage family, you reach the

unavoidable conclusion that as a society, we have stopped valuing our elderly...Yes, we could have more nurses, better nursing homes and accessible aged care services but you just have to talk to a patient to realise that none of it is a substitute for the investment of family. Fancy interventions and newer drugs will never be a proxy for the attentive kindness which is the strongest medicine of all.[7]

In this time of technological connectedness, loneliness is an epidemic.

The year after Britain voted to leave the European Union—thus becoming the metaphorical island it already is geographically—the country noted a serious problem with loneliness. According to a 2017 report published by the Jo Cox Commission on Loneliness, more than nine million people in the country often or always feel lonely.[8] Early in 2018, this prompted Prime Minister Theresa May to appoint a minister of loneliness.

"For far too many people, loneliness is the sad reality of modern life," Mrs. May said in a statement. "...people who have no one to talk to or share their thoughts and experiences with."

And the problem is not just in the UK.

Former US Surgeon General Murthy agreed loneliness is a growing health epidemic. Rates of loneliness have doubled since the 1980s. More than 40 percent of adults in America report feeling lonely, and research suggests the real number might be higher. In the workplace, many employees, and even more leaders, report feeling lonely in their roles:

> Loneliness and weak social connections are associated with a reduction in lifespan similar to that caused by smoking fifteen cigarettes a day and even greater than which associated with obesity. But we haven't focused nearly as much effort on strengthening connections between people as we have on curbing tobacco use or obesity. Loneliness is also associated with a greater risk of cardiovascular disease, dementia, depression, and anxiety. At work, loneliness limits creativity, and impairs other aspects of executive function such as reasoning and decision making. For our health and our work, it is imperative that we address the loneliness epidemic quickly.

> When we understand the profound human and economic costs of loneliness, we must determine whose responsibility it is to address the problem. The government and health care system have important roles to play in helping us understand the impact of loneliness, identifying who is affected, and determining which interventions work. But to truly solve loneliness requires the engagement of institutions where people spend the bulk of their time: families, schools, social organizations, and the workplace. Companies

in particular have the power to drive change at a societal level not only by strengthening connections among employees, partners, and clients but also by serving as an innovation hub that can inspire other organizations to address loneliness.

I believe the solution *starts* with you and with me. Standing up where people need us.

A simple touch of basic human decency may be what turns the tide of isolation, loneliness and divisiveness in our communities. When I really listen to what people across the political aisle from me say, I find we often are not far apart. We want our communities to be safe and our children to be well-educated and blessed. We don't want to see people suffer from homelessness, sickness, poverty or prejudice. We want the best for our fellow man.

When we stand face-to-face with people and operate in a community, we are more likely to try to find common ground and a solution that's amendable—or at least tolerable—for everyone. When we care, we all win.

We Must Appreciate Differences

While I'll admit I still have room to grow, I learned a great lesson—from a millennial, no less—a couple of years ago. We had a turnover of sales staff at Charlie Bravo Aviation, and Jake, our son, asked me if he could make some changes to that department.

I told him of the compensation negotiation struggles we'd had in the past, and he presented an idea I never would have conceived. Millennials have a reputation for being more collaborative than their parents—and his solution was in line with that. Jake's proposal created a fair compensation structure that benefits our clients more than the previous plan did and reduces contention between employees. Jake thinks differently than me, and it works.

One of the big arguments for having more female CEOs, board members, and managers within companies is that diversity of gender, risk aversion, problem-solving skills and cognitive thinking abilities balances decision making. Several reports, including one from Credit Suisse, indicate higher profitability correlating with women in positions of leadership.

You're likely not hiring CEOs or appointing board members regularly. However, if you're like me, you have the opportunity every day to squelch a stereotype and be open-minded about what others have to offer. Women's intuition should not be discounted.

One of my all-time favorite Disney movies is a newer classic—*Zootopia*. The setting of the movie is a world where predators and prey live in harmony, but prejudices still exist. One scene grips my heart. The scene opens with the protagonist Judy Hopps, a young rabbit, trying to make up for maligning her sidekick, a fox named Nick Wilde:

Judy Hopps: [*Searching for Nick on a small stone bridge over a ditch*] Nick? Nick?

[*leans over the edge, finding him sitting on a lawn chair below*]

Judy Hopps: Oh Nick! Night howlers aren't wolves! They're toxic flowers. I think someone is targeting predators on purpose and making them go savage.

Nick Wilde: [*Deadpan*] Wow. Isn't that interesting.

[*Nick gets up and walks under the bridge, while Judy follows him*]

Judy Hopps: Wait, uh, wait—listen! I - I know you'll never forgive me! And I don't blame you. I wouldn't forgive me either. I was ignorant, and... irresponsible... and small-minded. But predators shouldn't suffer because of my mistakes. I have to fix this.

[*Her voice shakes*]

Judy Hopps: But I can't do it without you.

[*Nick still refuses to turn around*]

Judy Hopps: [*Judy begins to cry*] And... and after we're done, you can hate me, and that'll be fine, because I was a horrible friend, and I hurt you. And you... and you can walk away

knowing you were right all along. I really am
just a dumb bunny.[1]

Judy misjudged Nick, misread the situation, and jeopardized their friendship. When she looked at the heart of the matter, she realized their differences combined made them stronger. They were able to right an injustice.

The movie was powerful because its release in March 2016 was a precursor to the volatile 2016 presidential election, one in which racial tensions were high and prejudices escalated.

When we open our eyes to the strengths of those around us and set our bigotry and prejudices aside, we can find common goals and impact the world around us. But we cannot just open our eyes. We must take action.

We Must Stand Up for What's Right

This is much, much easier said than done. Fear of being considered a hypocrite or politically incorrect has silenced many of us when we should be speaking out about injustices, crimes, terrorism and lack of respect.

In an October 2017 Twitter storm illuminating the sexist comments of another sports personality, ESPN Sunday Morning Countdown host Samantha Ponder defended her confrontation with the president of Barstool Sports.[2]

"I am speaking up not to say 'I am perfect, be like me' but rather 'where do we draw a line, what are our standards?' I don't meet my own standards sometimes. This does not mean we throw the standard away. This means we get better. We speak up. We listen. We get better. @sam_ponder"

We all have voices. It's time to use them. Even if they aren't perfect.

Our attitudes and values can create a healthy framework for the proper order of things. If we all use our voice and do our part, we can change the fabric of our society.

News headlines frequently highlight the lack of respect for authority in our communities. At times, our police officers must defend themselves against armed criminals resisting arrest, and we see looting, vandalizing, and people obstructing justice. We also see people dying in our streets and public meeting places. Racial tensions and hatred are escalating. We've all seen news footage showing blatant and mass disregard for law and authority. In these instances, we look more like a third-world country than the United States of America that our veterans fought and died to protect.

We say we want law and order, but do we give law enforcement officers the regard they deserve when we are pulled over? Are we not fostering lawlessness if we don't accept the citations we deserve and show lawmen and women, military and other public servants the respect that should come with their positions?

Beyond the streets, in our workplaces, a lack of respect has reduced productivity and profitability. Many employees don't think twice about shopping online, surfing Facebook, or sending personal emails even though they are being paid to work. These employees steal time they should be spending on business activities and likely erode their professional reputation in the process.

Showing up to work late, taking long lunches, and gossiping at the water cooler also show disregard for the urgency of company business. These behaviors, while they don't seem terrible, erode the foundation of a competitive advantage, putting companies unnecessarily at risk. It gets worse—some people disregard authority to the extent of embezzlement, fraud, and other criminal activities.

A gross lack of respect for authority has fueled mediocrity and worse in our schools. By staying silent about injustices in schools and encouraging our children to not rock the boat, we are guilty of perpetuating one of the most devastating injustices our society knows.

I consider bullying to be straight-up terrorism. Millions of teens contemplate suicide each year. The US Center for Disease Control and Prevention reports that 16 percent of high school teens have seriously considered suicide.[3] As a result, more than 4,600 young lives are lost each year. Bullying is a leading cause.

As a society we have become hypersensitive to hurting people's feelings. In our schools, parents have complained and complained so much about the way teachers have punished their children that it has restricted the schools' authority to discipline students. The lack of authority has allowed the "bad apples" to go unchecked, and now bullying is out of control. It's time to swing back the other direction.

Fostering a healthy respect for authority and other people creates environments with tremendous room for growth. These settings create champions and produce enviable legacies.

However, we cannot do this alone.

Everyone Needs Accountability

Each of us has blind spots, areas we cannot see, even though others around us can. Having people around who care enough to point out the hazards in business and life can help us avoid disasters. Sometimes admitting we are vulnerable, that we don't know it all or don't excel in everything, can lay the foundation for a great relationship. People like helping people. If someone projects that they never need help, they'll never get any. But those who seek help, guidance, or advice will find someone eager to be of assistance.

When we have room to celebrate each other's gifts and are willing to make each other better, we provide the environment for empowerment to take hold in our lives.

I find this kind of help in both formal and informal accountability. As I mentioned before, I am a part of a mastermind group that helps me form and implement both business and personal goals. The Women Presidents Organization groups me with businesswomen who are in various stages of business development and growth.

I have a few friends who have carte-blanche permission to call me out when I am behaving in a way contrary to what I've communicated are my ideals. I do the same for them. In our group, this ranges from not eating healthy to being taken advantage of by needy people to spending too much time on a work project that is not advantageous for our businesses.

In a recent lunch conversation, two of us told another friend that scheduling her date nights with her husband in fifteen-minute increments might be a tad controlling.

But we don't only identify each other's shortcomings. When we told our structured-date-night friend she needed to loosen up and set aside a day a month with *nothing* on the schedule, her eyes nearly popped out of her head. Spontaneity was a foreign concept to her, but she committed to embracing it.

As friends, we go the distance to provide or brainstorm solutions, often setting aside our own time to pitch in to help. There is no thought of the others being hypocrites, because we don't only want the best for each other. We work for it.

Confront in Love

We hear a lot these days about platform and influence. Finding a job, getting a publisher, being elected student council president—these all depend upon a positive social media or online presence. A hundred years ago, only a select few reporters, authors or politicians could reach a thousand people with their opinion. Today all of us can— and most of us do—on a daily basis. Our voices have a lot of volume.

Volume can be used for good or evil.

We are all guilty of hypocrisy—and we are likely guiltier of it than any other generation because our voices carry farther than ever before. But instead of pointing fingers at all the critics, bullies, racists, feminists, enablers, gossips, slanderers, and, yes, *sinners*, let's examine our own lives. But then, we should not live in fear of our inadequacies being exposed. We must work to be better and to help others. We can't watch someone walk off a cliff.

God gives us a blueprint on how to handle these things in Matthew 18:15-17. The same concept can work outside of church:

> If your brother or sister sins, go and point out their fault, just between the two of you. If they listen to you, you have won them over. But if they will not listen, take one or two others along, so that "every matter may be established by the testimony of two or three witnesses." If they still refuse to listen, tell it to the church; and if they refuse to listen even to the church, treat them as you would a pagan or a tax collector.

We should be leading the way in letting honor and grace and forgiveness and love and peace and patience guide us. We should exemplify Christ's qualities in a world that desperately needs them.

Rebutting someone's offensive post on Facebook with one of your own is protected by your First Amendment right to free speech if you are an American. However, as a Christ-follower, there's an additional standard by which we need to measure our speech.

We can lose the rewards, favor, and successes that God desires to bestow upon us by not honoring God, the authority in our lives, our spouses, or the people we lead.

We jeopardize blessings when we gripe about a co-worker, disdain authority, complain about our spouse or criticize a neighbor.

Are we supposed to ignore the things that are going on around us?

No.

If our desire is to have unity within our nation, an open and collaborative culture within our workplace, peace within our homes and fun instead of contention within our friendships, we have to set that example.

Perhaps we can learn from the example of a class of fifth graders at Bear Tavern Elementary in Titusville, New Jersey.[4] In 2017, the students heard the story of civil rights activist Reverend Gilbert Caldwell and his wife Grace. This African-American couple was denied the honeymoon they planned by a prejudiced front desk clerk at Mount Airy Resort in the Poconos of Pennsylvania sixty years ago.

The Caldwells have recounted the story a hundred times in different settings as part of a presentation on the civil rights movement. But when this group of fifth graders heard the speech, they decided to take action. Each student wrote to the management of the resort, which is now under new ownership, asking for a honeymoon re-do.

One of the students said the Caldwells "made me think about not only standing up for myself, but standing up for others and fixing mistakes that were made in the world." If only we could all be as brave as twelve-year-olds.

In *Crucial Conversations: Tools for Talking When Stakes Are High*, authors Kerry Patterson, Joseph Grenny, Ron McMillan and Al Switzler establish conversations as crucial when opinions vary, emotions run strong and much is at risk:

> When it comes to risky, controversial, and emotional conversations, skilled people find a way to get all relevant information (from themselves and others) out into the open. That's it. At the core of every successful conversation lies the free flow of relevant information. People openly and honestly express their opinions, share their feelings, and articulate their theories. They willingly and capably share their views, even when their ideas are controversial or unpopular. It's the one thing that…extremely effective communicators we studied were routinely able to achieve. Now to put a label on this spectacular talent—it's called dialogue.[5]

As leaders, we should be engaging in dialogue and leading the way in letting honor and grace and forgiveness and love and peace and patience guide us. We should not cower and remain quiet. We must confront the things we believe are wrong in our world if we want to make it a better place for our children and their children. This is possible, and in the attempt, we exemplify Christ's qualities in a world that desperately needs them.

We Need Help

I'm not diminishing the difficulty of practicing what we preach. Even the Apostle Paul admitted to struggling with this in his letter to the Romans:

> What I don't understand about myself is that I decide one way, but then I act another, doing things I absolutely despise. If I can't be trusted to figure out what is best for myself and then do it, it becomes obvious God's command is necessary.

> But I need something *more*! For if I know the law but still can't keep it, and if the power of sin within me keeps sabotaging my best intentions, I obviously need help. I realize I don't have what it takes. I can will it, but I can't *do* it. I decide to do good, but I don't *really* do it; I decide not to do bad, but then I do it anyway. My decisions, such as they are, don't result in actions. Something has gone wrong deep within me and gets the better of me every time (Rom. 7:15-20, MSG).

He may have written the words two thousand years ago, but they ring so true to me, I could have written them myself. We all need help. Sometimes it is external. Sometimes it comes from within.

I find that if I think about positive things, my actions and conversation follow the lead. One of my favorite scriptures is Philippians 4:8… and it is followed by a verse well-known among athletes: Philippians 4:13. "I can do all things through Christ who strengthens me." This means, through His strength, I can stay focused on things true, noble, right, pure, lovely, admirable, excellent or praiseworthy.

From that moment of conviction behind the lady in the Women of Faith conference, I learned I cannot judge someone by appearances only. From learning to appreciate what others bring to the table and giving others permission to correct me when I get off-course, I learned I can live a richer life.

I can change and grow.

I can live a life of excellence, caring about and for the people around me, without having my life scream that I'm a hypocrite—although I'm pretty sure I, like the Apostle Paul, still have those tendencies.

Chapter 8

Aligning Your Future

O n my most difficult days, I want to be successful at something. Anything. I don't care what it is. It can be getting the laundry done without any unmatched socks. Or forgetting an ingredient and having dinner turn out okay anyway. Or closing a sale when it feels like everything else in my life is spiraling out of control.

This is where planning for success and journaling comes in for me. It's how I avoid the panic of not getting important things done and wasting my days away because I just don't feel like doing things.

Journaling has become as important a part of my morning as drinking coffee. I start by reflecting on what I did and learned the day before and writing down the things for which I am most grateful at that moment, and I end with some thought to how I might spend my day. On the weekends, it might be a whole list of things, or just one important task.

During the week, I try to identify three things that will move a project or goal along. I base these on my goals for the week, which are structured around quarterly or annual milestones. Often these strategic tasks take less than twenty or thirty minutes, but they all add up at the end of the day, week or month. And they give me a sense of peace and accomplishment during the week, whether that week is hectic and jam-packed or it's one where I am mostly waiting for things to fall into place.

I know we cannot win at everything every day. But we can make significant progress on the things that matter most. This is possible even when the stakes are high or we've been dealt a hand we don't like. The rise of the underdog makes a great hero's story.

Millions of dollars in cash on the table and the backstory of ordinary people winning and losing make the World Series of Poker a popular ESPN viewing event.

But sitting in front of the television with an insider's view of the cards in each player's hand hardly portrays the stress of sitting at the green, felt-covered table with opponents—and cameras—scrutinizing your every weakness. Nerve-wracking as it may be to sit at the table, playing your hand right requires focus. And walking away takes courage.

Annie Duke, one of poker's most celebrated female players, describes it this way in her book *How I Raised, Folded, Bluffed, Flirted, Cursed, and Won Millions at the World Series of Poker*:

> In poker, as in life, you've got to know what you need in order to succeed. Sometimes, it's obvious. New players can't hope to win at poker without understanding the statistical odds of a

hand or the importance of betting position to your play... But often it's not easy to identify what it is that's stalling you. It might not be obvious that you're losing hands because you've stopped paying attention to the patterns in your opponents' play, that what you might need is to take a brisk walk around the block to get out of your own way, or to just call it a night.[1]

Duke describes leaving the tournament table in 2004 to find a cash game to win, one where the stakes are a little lower, to rebuild her confidence and regain control of emotions that could derail her plans to win the most prestigious title in professional poker. Unknown to her opponents, her stress was compounded by an imminent divorce. She pulled herself together and won the title.

Often, when we find ourselves in a highly volatile situation, a step back, a pep-talk from someone we trust, an easy confidence boost or a renewed enthusiasm help us cross the finish line well. When we pause, any of those things could help us find a solution—or more importantly identify other considerations that could affect the outcome.

One of my favorite Bible characters epitomizes this approach. She was poor. Jewish. Female. An orphan. To make matters more intriguing, Esther was not playing a game with pride and millions of dollars at stake—although those things did come into play. She gambled her *life* for the chance to save the entire nation of Israel from annihilation.

Before her defining moment, Esther found sufficient favor with King Xerxes to be made his queen. But Xerxes was a loose cannon, easily influenced by his advisors, and subject to his own follies as dictated by the law of the Medes and Persians.

While he honored Esther by making her queen, at the time when the news of impending doom reached her, Xerxes had not summoned her in thirty days. I imagine she felt as though she had been put out to pasture, a subject of Xerxes' well-documented capriciousness.

Her uncle and advisor Mordecai suggested she plead for the lives of her countrymen, a heritage of which the king was unaware. She panicked and refused. Mordecai pressed her. "If you remain silent at this time, relief and deliverance for the Jews will arise from another place, but you and your father's family will perish. And who knows but that you have come to your royal position for such a time as this?" (Est. 4:14).

At her defining moment, Esther took a pause and asked Mordecai to have all the Jews in Susa do the same. They fasted and sought the Lord for three days before Esther appeared unsummoned before the king, which was against the law.

Dressed in her royal finery, with courage from above, she approached the throne. Xerxes extended his golden scepter, staying his bodyguards, a.k.a. executioners. He was so pleased by Queen Esther's appearance he offered her anything, up to half the kingdom.

Equipped with the knowledge of the law and an assessment of her opponent's (and husband's) character, Esther requested a meal with the king and Haman, the king's advisor who had ordered the obliteration of the Jews. At the banquet, she requested nothing more than an audience with the king and Haman again the next night.

Who but God could have imagined the turn of events in the next twenty-four hours? The king could not sleep and asked for a servant to read him records. Mordecai was recognized for past heroism. Haman was humiliated, confronted and hanged. A new law said Jews could defend themselves. Esther was given Haman's immense financial holdings. And Mordecai replaced Haman as chief advisor to the king.

The lessons I draw from Esther and other contemporary leaders make the foundation of my success.

I've learned the aggressor doesn't always win. If I bide my time, prepare my heart, and seek God's glory, my stress decreases and my successes build on one another.

Align with What God Wants

What I really want is to have a greater overall success rate. I figured out early on in my walk with God how to accomplish this. And I have forgotten it over and over again in my quest for a successful life. Keeping the concept front-of-mind requires concentration—and an active prayer life.

We are selfish creatures, often out of alignment with God's purpose for our lives. When we figure out His purpose, the things for which we ask fall in line with what God wants for us.

The secret to knowing what God wants is a two-way dialogue. I achieve this by reading and studying the Bible, making my requests known to God, and journaling. I find if I write out my prayers out, even though it goes more slowly, I get clarity about things. Writing also allows me the reality check of "hearing" what I'm asking for.

If I want to convince Curt about something, I might pray out loud "Lord, he's so bull headed. Why can't he see things my way?" But when I start writing, it morphs to "Lord, I really want Curt to understand where I am coming from. Help me to understand his hesitation. Help us not fall prey to the ploys of division but have a spirit of unity."

Prayer also helps shift our focus from ourselves to others, which, in turn drives out any lingering self-pity. I've learned to do this over the years by going back and reading my old prayer journals and feeling ashamed at some of the pettier things I've written. Journaling has not only kept me on track, it has matured my faith and my prayer life.

Be Patient

I still forget to pray about things sometimes and get carried away with making my own decisions. I blaze full steam ahead with my own ideas about how to accomplish the things I believe God has for me. Sometimes there's no harm done, but other times, the action triggers deep regret.

One of the biggest areas where women get caught in this trap is with their husbands. An old adage often rings true: Men marry hoping their wives will never change. Women marry hoping they can change their husbands. I have found this to be spot on when I've talked with other wives, no matter how long they've been married.

We can't help ourselves. We all want our husbands to be everything God created them to be. If we are working out or eating right every day, we want them to be doing the same and reaping the same benefits. However, we cannot force this. For one thing, everyone has his or her own journey to walk.

The other reason this approach fails is this: we are not the Holy Spirit. We cannot convict another of their shortcomings effectively. I'd be embarrassed to count how many times I've been journaling and the thought pop into my head that I was trying to do God's job. When I quit striving and trust him to accomplish His purposes without my help (or perhaps interference), things happen.

Remember when you taught a child to tie their shoes? They might be slower or tie a bundle of knots, but if you let them figure it out, they'll do it well before long.

I remember Curt getting frustrated with Brooke when she was in elementary school. "Can you please get her to do something with her hair? It has no style."

My response was that it was clean and brushed.

Less than two years later, Curt's frustration shifted. "Why is Brooke not ready yet? Is she still in the bathroom doing her hair? How long can it possibly take?"

The same thing applies with developing a relationship with God. We cannot force anyone else's salvation or maturity. And our patience here may take a lifetime—and a lot of diligent prayer.

If we want to experience supernatural results, like Esther, we must trust God to do His thing.

We Must Know When to Ask

In business, in life, and in prayer, we must know when to ask. Using Esther as an example, we should know what we want, who can grant it, what that person's weaknesses or expectations are, and the most conducive environment and timing for the person you are asking to say yes.

Esther knew she wanted Xerxes to save her people. She also knew the law that condemned them could not be reversed. She knew the previous queen had been deposed because she embarrassed Xerxes in public. And she knew that, unless she exposed Haman, he would figure out a way to undo anything she accomplished. She didn't lose her nerve the first night. She acted strategically.

At a pivotal point in our marriage, I knew Curt and I needed to have a deep conversation to bring us back into alignment with one another. I knew from twenty-five years of experience that it wouldn't be an easy talk. My goal was to get him to participate in a study on marriage, which several friends had recommended. They said it facilitated conversations within their marriages.

I knew I couldn't ask first thing in the morning, or after a few cocktails in the evening. Instead of plowing ahead with my own timing, I waited several months for an opportune moment. I introduced Curt to a friend who invited him to race Lamborghinis on the Austin Formula One track. The day after the race, he was still on an adrenaline rush, grinning from ear-to-ear when I asked.

"Hey, honey, I'm so glad you had a good time racing. It makes me happy to see you this excited about something.

I feel like that spark has been missing." When he agreed, I moved in: "I think our marriage could use a spark like that too. What do you think about taking this assessment and maybe going through this book several people recommended?"

Not only did he say yes, but the resulting conversations led to the greater emotional intimacy I wanted.

I've also learned how to apply this patient strategy in business. Airplane sales may seem straightforward, but when you are dealing with lots of money, international laws, grey areas of airworthiness conditions, and big personalities, things can get heated. At work, I am the person who takes the transaction from concept—a signed letter of intent— through to the closing. I frequently "re-close" a deal five or six times before the commission is in the bank.

This requires exceptional listening skills and an ability to identify the biggest underlying objectives. Is money the sticking point, or is meeting the deadline critical because there's an important trip looming? Closing also involves out-of-the-box thinking. I can't tell you how many times I've been able to save a sale because I used a personal connection to make something happen at the last minute.

I also have learned to ask boldly for the things I need. The worst that can happen is they say no. The best result is being part of a miracle for someone who needs one.

Years ago, when fires ravaged the Bastrop, Texas, area, I learned about several aid organizations that were sending eighteen-wheelers to our area with supplies. The outreach pastor at our church said he needed some place to receive those items and store them until the victims were settled enough to use them. He said it would be nice to have a warehouse and a loading dock.

I called my neighbor, who was also the city manager, and asked if the city still owned the old Albertson's grocery store building. He confirmed it did. I asked if we could use it for relief work. He said yes. Then I asked if we could start using it right away, because two trucks were in route. I knew I was pushing it. We met at the store, and I talked him into turning on the electricity and providing keys in less than an hour. I worked within the fire code restrictions by countering his hesitations with creative solutions. I was operating in line with what I now know to be my underlying purpose—and I found it gratifying.

To get what we want, we must know how to ask, when to ask, who to ask, and how to be bold in the asking. But sometimes, that's not enough.

We Have Authority

I think God allows my job to become extremely frustrating so I can experience "aha" moments.

After one particularly trying day with an international transaction, our pastor Joe Champion was at our house for dinner. Rather flippantly, he asked, "Sell any planes today?"

I told him of the latest fiasco. He counseled some things only move with prayer and fasting. Tried that. He said even Daniel's prayers went unanswered for a time because of demonic opposition. I empathized. He then said something that would come back to mind several days later.

"God says, 'Command ye me.'"

I wondered, who am I to command God? I searched my Bible and couldn't find the precedent. Finally, I typed the words into my web browser. The results only came up in older versions of Isaiah 45:11, like the King James Version, which states, "Thus saith the Lord...concerning the work of my hands command ye me."

In the NIV, the passage was "do you give me orders about the work of my hands?" And in The Message, it read, "Are you telling me what I can or cannot do?"

I was confused, but I was desperate for a breakthrough, so I asked God to help me find answers about commanding. Immediately, He prompted me to pray as Jesus prayed. I turned to the Lord's Prayer, which is where Jesus instructed the disciples who were in the same frustrated conundrum as me.

"Give us this day..." Give us. A command. I had my answer. I changed my prayers. I wrote it out, so I wouldn't forget the power I felt surging through my veins at the time. And it was a turning point for me.

I'll share a bit of it here, so you can see how different it is from, "Lord, please bless us, but if it's not your will right now, I'll live with that." There's nothing wrong with that sentiment, but what God was trying to teach me in this season was the access I have to His power through His promises.

I pray His own Word back to Him. Here it is:

In Isaiah 45, You say to declare what is to be.

I declare my toils have not been made in vain (1 Cor. 15:58). I declare the work of my hands will yield a harvest, of 30 or 60 or even 100-fold (Matt. 13:8). I declare that which has been withheld will be released. I declare the floodgates will open and the mercies and provision of God will stream forward (Mal. 3:10).

You will use everything I have poured my energy into. You will level the mountains before me (Isa. 45:2) and make my path straight (Pro. 3:6). You will cause my enemies to fall into their own traps (Psa. 31:4). You will destroy those who seek to destroy me (Psa. 63:9). Even if I feel hard-pressed or overwhelmed, I am not crushed (2 Cor. 4:8).

You will sustain me. You will bring to pass the plans You have for me (Pro. 19:21)...plans for a hope and a future (Jer. 29:11). Plans for strength and fruitfulness, plans for victory and not defeat (1 John 5:4). I shall shout for joy over your victory, oh God.

Lord, your Word says I have power and authority (Luke 10:9). Your Word says I should command You (Isa. 45:11) concerning my provision—and then Jesus reinforces that in the Lord's Prayer when He says, "give us this day our daily bread" (Matt. 6:11).

Today, I claim the power you have vested in me, and I break the hold the enemy has over our finances. I demolish the strongholds; I demolish the arguments against me and my family and company. I demolish the arguments against my relationship with You. (2 Cor 10:4-5) I take charge of the things over which You have given me power and authority, and I declare them to be so. Amen.

Declaring these things has shifted everything for me. Not only did it bolster my confidence in prayer, but it changed the way I looked at myself. When you believe you have power and authority, you carry yourself differently.

This may be a simple illustration, but I have season tickets to a local sporting event, and my seats are on the floor, right by the visitors' bench. Most people are stopped on their way through the passageway to the floor seats, but I just walk on through. I know I belong there—and the security guards either know who I am or they recognize the confidence I carry and don't bother me.

The same concept rings true spiritually, and with bigger implications. When I conduct myself with authority, I have a greater impact on the world around me. Don't just stand up. Walk it out.

Chapter 9

Conquering Fears

I have a ninety-five-pound American Bulldog named Bazooka. This is a breed recognized for its strength, stoicism and protectiveness. He indeed has a ferocious bark and a menacing profile, yet Bazooka is a snuggler and often appears more fearful than fearsome. When someone wears a hat or carries in a plant, Bazooka retreats. If something new is on the patio, he will refuse to go out, even to play.

This tough, intimidating pup tucks his tail and backs away at the sight of a mop bucket, and, no, I don't think it's a male gender bias. I've often wondered how this bucket-fearing puppy terrifies an African dinner guest who is seven feet tall and weighs 250 pounds. I found it ironic that this guy who slams buckets for a living as a professional basketball player is afraid of a dog that's afraid of mop buckets. But in all fairness, our dinner guest grew up in a region of the world where big dogs are wild animals, not domesticated house pets.

While a fear of buckets or dogs is not likely to derail you, some fears will. And your reaction to them is real.

The response to a perceived harmful event, or threat to survival is a physiological reaction priming an animal for fighting or fleeing. We don't live in a jungle; we live in a civilized world. Most of our fears aren't because of threats to our survival. Regardless of what we've been through, how strong we are, or what we know, we're all afraid of something. Our fears can result from actual experiences or they can be born from our insecurities. No one is immune. We all fear different things. Some fear is healthy. It restrains us from danger. Some fears, however, are unfounded.

Our fears are more mental or emotional. Our imagination takes us to a possible future where the worst has happened and we are humiliated or impoverished somehow. These fears cause many of us to flee or freeze, to either run away from our calling or remain stagnant. But some things are certainly worth fighting for.

We may choose to refrain from bad behavior because we fear getting in trouble. We may make better financial decisions because we fear poverty or not having money for retirement or emergencies. We may tell the truth because we know God will expose a lie. He says the "fear of the Lord is the beginning of wisdom."

But fear should not paralyze us. We can conquer fears. We can use that fear, which releases adrenaline, to make us sharper in a deadly or defining moment. The Bible says we are more than conquerors, and I believe fear is something that can be and should be conquered. When we are walking in line with His will, we are ensured the victory in the end, no matter how much the odds are stacked against us.

"He who has overcome his fears will truly be free."

–Aristotle

Reverse the Fear of Rejection

When I was a kid, I sold Girl Scout cookies door-to-door. I'd canvas the neighborhood in my uniform with the little green sash, proudly displaying my badged accomplishments. Most neighbors would invite me in, order a few boxes, and ask how school was going. Nobody was carb-conscious or gluten-free back then. Friendly neighbors ordered at least one box, and if they didn't want cookies, they typically didn't answer the door.

Today, Girl Scouts get a first-hand taste of what it feels like to have a real sales job. Because of changing policies, instead of canvassing their neighborhoods, they now must stand in front of a local retailer with a table and a couple of moms, with boxes and boxes of cookies to sell to all who pass by.

Those of us who have already bought five boxes and hidden them in the freezer, so our husband doesn't get into them might enter a different door to avoid the table. Or we might say, "no, we've already bought some," or we might avoid eye contact altogether. Maybe we tell them we will buy some on the way out, and then conveniently forget or wait for others to exit so we can sneak by in the crowd. We can't imagine what some of those shy little darlings think when their turn comes up to man the sales table. But that pressure—and yes, even rejection—prepares Girl Scouts to handle adult situations early on.

In higher-stakes sales jobs, we face some of the same obstacles the Girl Scouts do. People avoid us, screen calls, have someone else run interference or say no before we make our presentation. Selling big-ticket items that involve prospecting sometimes means a thousand negative responses before there is one resulting in a commission check. That's a lot of rejection.

While you'll certainly avoid rejection if you don't ask, that fear can limit the positive responses to absolutely zilch. Girl Scouts don't quit because someone doesn't buy cookies. They learn how to handle the negative and keep going despite the rejection. Facing the fear of rejection builds confidence. If Girl Scouts can face it, we can as well. The stakes might be higher, but the rewards are too.

If fear of rejection is an issue for you, surround yourself with people who can help you overcome this fear. This type of fear is a killer because your future is at stake. Finding or building community is the best place to find supportive people.

We need to be aware, as parents, that our fear of rejection can project itself onto our kids. Our lack of confidence handicaps them in the classroom, on the playground, and in difficult situations.

As business leaders, we can cripple our coworkers by stifling enthusiasm and the willingness to take risks. Eventually, we must choose to manage rejection from other people instead of compromising our dreams or failing to fulfill our purpose.

Rejection poses difficult challenges, especially if you're a recovering perfectionist like me. I'm not sure how Curt survived the early days of our marriage. I burst into tears and shut him out at the slightest provocation.

If he didn't tell me he liked a dinner I prepared, I would ask, fishing for a compliment. Trying to be honest but not wanting to hurt my feelings, he sometimes said something like, "it isn't my favorite." Which I somehow twisted into "*you're* not my favorite." I was crushed. I felt like an inadequate wife. And I turned a cold shoulder to my husband who was being honest.

I am embarrassed to count how many years it took me to respond instead with "I didn't really like it that much either," or "there's cereal in the pantry if you want something else." The first step to recovering from rejection is to separate the offensive statement or action from your own personal value.

In the instance of the meal, Curt was not rejecting me. He merely stated his preference, based on his taste buds. It had nothing to do with me as a person.

Developing discernment and a thicker skin also helped me cope with the rejection in sales. I can now ask why someone is rejecting an airplane or my services and handle the answer. I filter it through experience and sometimes come up with a different answer than what that person presented.

Many times, "it's overpriced" means "I can't afford it." Or "it hasn't been well-maintained; the paint is chipping" translates to "I don't really know what I'm examining." Look beneath the surface. Sometimes ego exudes rejection. As a woman in a man's world, I've learned to allow a client's pride to remain intact while repelling criticism. I separate the rejection from the value of my product or person.

You also must reject the rejection. It may sound silly, but self-talk is the best way to accomplish this. Remind yourself of your purpose. Of what God says about you. Of the promise others have seen in you.

Frame letters of recommendation and hang them in a prominent place. Print and display quotes or memes that uplift you. Create screen savers of nice things people have said about you. Download an app that allows you to record uplifting statements, which play back for you at certain times of the day. Be who you are supposed to be. Unapologetically.

Push past it. Get over it. Move on. Don't let rejection define you.

Others' Opinions Can't Derail Us

Author and speaker Lisa Bevere is one of the boldest people I know. She speaks out about injustices. She also champions women in countries where it's unpopular to promote women's rights. And she fearlessly tells it like she sees it. But that wasn't always the case.

Lisa's story is one of overcoming her fears. In high school, she was required to take either speech or debate to graduate. No prospect could have frightened her more. She has said, "As a teenager, I was terrified of getting up in front of people. I had lost an eye to a form of cancer called retinoblastoma when I was five years old. Overnight, life as I'd known it changed. I went from being confident and outgoing to being sullen and withdrawn. I felt people no longer saw me. I watched as they tried to determine which eye they should look at when they spoke to me. At school, compliments changed to name-calling. I was dubbed 'One Eye' and 'Cyclops.'"

The day she had to give her first speech in high school was a disaster. Her fear paralyzed her voice box. The teacher gave her the opportunity to walk out of the classroom and start again, but she chose not to. Instead, she ran to the guidance counselor's office. He was sympathetic to Lisa's handicap, and not just for speech class. He also let her opt out of typing, which was difficult with limited vision.

She had study hall instead of typing and a literature course in the place of speech class, but the avoidance didn't last forever. When she became an adult, she ended up learning the lessons in a much tougher environment, a stage onto which her loving husband repeatedly pushed her, one that eventually helped her overcome her fears.

Today, as the best-selling author of more than a dozen books (all of which she typed herself) and as one of the most highly sought-after female Christian speakers in the world, Lisa is pretty much fearless. Nobody looks more comfortable on stage than Lisa Bevere. She faced her fear of public speaking, her fear of looking foolish, her fear of being the focus of people's attention, even when she could only focus on them with one eye. The fear that finally drove Lisa to succeed was the fear that she would miss her destiny.

Don't we owe it to ourselves to learn the opinion of the One who created us rather than that of the many naysayers who don't know our potential?

We Must Believe Change can be Good

Dr. Spencer Johnson's book *Who Moved My Cheese?* is an encouraging and thought-provoking resource for those facing change. It's a parable that shows how four different characters handle a shift in resources. The two mice, Sniff and Scurry, remain nimble and handle the depletion of their cheese supply without much angst. The two little people, Hem and Haw, with a reasonable supply, become complacent, build a life around their resources, and delay making changes when their circumstances change.

The book is a lighthearted exposé on the different reactions to change and how we can handle them appropriately. It's an easy read, and with more than 26,000,000 copies sold worldwide, you should be able to find a copy in your local library or maybe on the bookshelf of a friend who has navigated a transition.

Change isn't always bad, even when it appears to be. Being able to adapt to new circumstances is a trait you should develop.

In 2002, Curt and I moved our family from the Washington, D.C. area to a suburb of Austin, Texas. He wanted to sell airplanes, and the job opportunity there showed promise. I remember calling my cousins who remained on the East Coast to tell them we were seventeen miles from the closest Target. Six kinds of livestock roamed behind fences on my way to the nearest Starbucks. And there were tarantulas. As big as my hand with my fingers spread out. Hairy. Spiders. Not okay.

If you've ever moved across the country or to a different country altogether, you know environmental changes aren't the biggest adjustments. There are some emotional hurdles as well. Curt and I had finally moved far enough away that I couldn't jump in the car and drive to my mom's comforting sweet rolls any time things got tense with my husband or I was feeling homesick.

I was in my thirties and shouldn't have needed my mom so much, but I still felt a little bereft at the thought of not seeing her as often. I had to choose a new pediatrician on my own, figure out the best grocery stores, and make new friends.

But we left D.C. after 9/11 and one day before authorities caught the sniper who terrorized the entire metroplex for weeks. The move was a good one, allowing us to grow closer as a family, build new careers, and become part of a vibrant, growing community. We grew roots. We made friends we count as family. Now when people ask where we are from, we don't say we live in Texas. We say we are Texans. It's in our blood.

When you finally face your fears, you realize the worst thing that can happen is missing the opportunities that give your life significance. Those things that influence, empower, encourage, or motivate others to emulate your example are far more important than fear, no matter how real or big your fears may seem.

Like Lisa Bevere, you must harness the power of your fears into something positive. That's what got me on stage the very first time.

You must turn the fear of rejection into determination not to take no for an answer. Decide that quitting is not an option. Get excited that change can fuel new opportunities. Your life story doesn't have to be dictated by anyone's opinion of you. Do not fear criticism—and when you do, pull strength from one of the most famous writers of our day.

"I've heard there are troubles of more than one kind; some come from ahead, and some come from behind. But I've brought a big bat. I'm all ready, you see; now my troubles are going to have troubles with me!" –Dr. Seuss

Chapter 10
Finding Purpose

L ife produces unexpected twists and turns, but they all seem to end up creating one long interconnected and interesting journey. Finding your way often depends on finding your why. Both your way and your why can pivot as you grow. The "ways" turn by 90 and 180 degrees. The "whys" make subtle shifts. Mine sure did.

How did I go from being a car-pool driving, stay-at-home mom to being one of the most recognized female private jet brokers in the world? I wish I could say I woke up one morning with the dream, thought it sounded easy, and executed a three-step formula you could repeat. But alas, as you now know, mine is a story of disappointments, adversity, marital conflicts, fear, loneliness and failures—along with a few personal victories, big paydays, and very interesting opportunities.

Through the professional and personal struggles I've shared, I've found a new side of myself, one where I relish making what seems impossible possible. The way I accomplish my why has changed. The why is nearly the same. Every day I get to look beyond the stated sales objections to the underlying motivations in clients or opponents from a myriad of cultures and legal jurisdictions. It's a happy day when I find a way forward where others gave up or outright failed, because my why is to help people come up with creative solutions.

In the cutthroat, 99 percent male world of private jet brokerage, with millions of dollars at stake and no regulations to govern competition, I've been knocked down a few times. I've been excluded from conversations and associations because of my gender. As a small business owner in a prolonged financial downturn, I've spent sleepless nights wondering how I would make payroll. But I've prevailed despite the difficulties by leaning in when I really feel like shrinking back and standing when I'd rather be disappearing. So I can live my why.

Perhaps, after nearly thirty years of marriage, my husband's tenacity has rubbed off on me. Or maybe I've found that when I stand for something, I can see more clearly. React better. Pivot to a more advantageous position.

Standing is the key. Both physically and metaphorically, standing is a position of readiness and leadership. I've had to find the courage to stand up. Stand out. And stand firm in my personal beliefs and my faith.

On the upside, I've formed friendships with celebrities, dignitaries and unsung heroes who are saving the world. I've participated in disaster relief efforts that saved lives in Haiti, Louisiana and Texas. And I've had the opportunity to share my faith with influencers who may not have heard it from anyone else—again, by standing up when I feel more like curling up on my couch.

There's a lot more grit than glamour in my life, notwithstanding the interesting stories in my social media feeds. In my darkest days, I hold on to hope and faith despite the doubts that come with being thrust into an unexpected role.

I would not change anything about my story—especially if my insights have helped you write yours a little stronger, a little bolder, or a little richer. As I've said before, my deepest desire is to see those whose lives mine has touched live to see and believe their own potential.

To believe in yourself, you first must know who you were created to be—and then believe in the possibility that you can be that person. No matter the circumstances you're in right now. No matter the choices you've made. No matter what others say about you. It is possible.

You May Need Your ID Card Renewed

My foundational belief in who I am lies in what God has to say about me and the world around me. Circumstances change. Mine did. Some of those changes were painful. But I am still the same person underneath. You also are who God made you to be, no matter what that looks like.

My heart breaks with the thought that you may be living lonely, depressed, brokenhearted, insecure, unloved, addicted, abused, poverty stricken, or helpless. If you look in the Bible, there is relief—and it is the place I find my best encouragement. In the gospel of John, Jesus tells us He came so we could truly live life to its fullest, not survive in drudgery. Jesus sacrificed His life so I could live as His sister, with all the benefits of that royal family. The same promise is available to any who believe in Him. This means we are:

Free.

Planned.

Designed for a purpose.

Redeemed.

Loved.

Cherished.

Beautiful.

Conquerors.

Warriors.

Adopted.

Saved.

Precious.

Victorious.

Sometimes I struggle to identify with any of those descriptors, let alone all of them. I know I'm not the only one. Perhaps that's because we live in—and seem to be defined by—an era that promotes constant busyness and performance, never-ending visual comparison, and pressures unlike those of any generation before us. Unless a crisis sends us to our knees, to a counselor, or to aisle after aisle of self-help books, we rarely pause to assess who we are.

Then, when we do examine ourselves, we put increasing pressure on ourselves to realign our priorities, quit bad habits, or "try to be better." Instead of being assured of our identity, this evaluation seems to make life even harder and drags us deeper into a pit of self-condemnation or self-pity.

I navigate my way through these periods by using what some would call the power of positive thinking. My redirect is based on Philippians 4:8, which says, "whatever is true, whatever is noble, whatever is right, whatever is pure, whatever is lovely, whatever is admirable—if anything is excellent or praiseworthy—think about such things." Some days, I have to put the verse on a sticky note on my computer screen.

Other days, I must rely on someone else to remind me. If I didn't have sisters, friends, parents and pastors speaking life and encouragement in the days I feel weakest and most defeated, I would be nothing more than weak or defeated. In turn, I try to do that in their lives.

Understand Your Superpowers

I am a big fan of action-adventure movies—especially those with superheroes. My family sometimes talks about favorite powers at dinner. If you could have one superpower, what would it be?

With as much time as I spend commuting or traveling, I would choose the ability to teleport. To see a natural wonder or be with someone when they needed me most—and not just through television or FaceTime—would be heavenly. Maybe you'd rather have another power, but I bet you'd pick something cool.

I love the T-shirt that shows Batman, Spider-Man, Ironman, Captain America, The Incredible Hulk, Flash, and Superman on a ledge with Jesus. The conversation bubble above Jesus' head says, "and that's how I saved the world." Had I made the shirt, I would have added a few female superheroes, but my point is the same—Jesus did save the world. And then He ascended to heaven and left us with the superpowers He used to do it.

While they aren't fodder for Hollywood's superhero movies, I think they're applicable to the battles we face today.

We don't have X-ray vision. We have spiritual discernment.

We don't become stronger when we are angry. We trust God's strength is made perfect in our weakness, thereby giving us the power to move mountains and raise the dead.

We don't need a superhero organization at our beck and call. We have the personal contact details for the King of the Universe.

We can't create a spiderweb. We can pray for and see miracles.

Christians have access to this power. But we don't get full access all at once. Not even movie superheroes do. The ability to use our power increases incrementally as we grow. And there are some keys we need to use for access to more peace, more influence, more credibility in our faith, more success, more power, more favor. With our families. At our workplaces. In our faith.

So how do I get these superpowers? I ask for them. In James 4, I am told I do not have because I do not ask. If I ask and do not receive, it is because I ask that I may spend what I receive on my own pleasure. Ouch. I guess that means superpowers are not for the selfish.

God does not give us superpowers so we can get revenge on a bully or win a competition. He equips us supernaturally to build His kingdom here on earth, to strengthen and encourage His church and the people in it. If we want to be powerful, supernaturally so, we must align ourselves with what He wants us to be. Or as my husband says in a redneck accent when someone has a lousy golf game, "well, bless his heart, he just needs to get his towards right." We must find what some call our true north. Our purpose. Or rather, His purpose for us.

The most popular book of all time regarding purpose is Rick Warren's *Purpose Driven Life.* Warren starts his book with two quotations. The first is from atheist Bertrand Russell: "Unless you assume a God, the question of life's purpose is meaningless." The second quote is Colossians 1:16 from the Message translation of the Bible: "For everything, absolutely everything, above and below, visible and invisible … everything got started in [God] and finds its purpose in him."

Warren goes on to say our purpose is not about us:

The search for the purpose of life has puzzled people for thousands of years. That's because we typically begin at the wrong starting point—ourselves. We ask self-centered questions like what do *I* want to be? What should *I* do with *my* life? What are *my* goals, *my* ambitions, *my* dreams for *my* future? But focusing on ourselves will never reveal our life's purpose. [1]

Our best purpose aligns with what God has in mind for us, whatever that may be. Our job is to discover our God-designed purpose and fulfill it.

Define Your Purpose

The importance of finding purpose is not only a Christian ideal. It's scientific. According to the Association for Psychological Science, developing a sense of purpose may add years to your life. In 2014, Patrick Hill of Carleton University in Canada and Nicholas Turiano of the University of Rochester Medical Center studied more than 6,000 people and did a follow-up fourteen years later.[2] They concluded that those who reported a greater sense of purpose and direction in life were more likely to outlive their peers.

Hill said, "Our findings point to the fact that finding direction for life, and setting overarching goals for what you want to achieve can help you actually live longer, regardless of when you find your purpose. So the earlier someone comes to a direction for life, the earlier these protective effects may be able to occur."

I believe I have a specific calling, just as I believe you are on this earth for a unique purpose—to share your gifts, talents, skills, and life experiences. This is key to getting us out of bed in the morning and continuing in the face of adversity. It also awards us the greatest sense of accomplishment (a.k.a. kicking-tail-and-taking-names days).

You may not know what your purpose is or how to pursue it, but the world is missing out on something if you are unable or unwilling to discover and fulfill it. No matter who you are, you have a legacy to leave.

Unless you are intentional about your purpose, you slide toward *living a life without purpose*. Without purpose, you may feel aimless, chaotic, pointless, random, indecisive, fruitless, impotent, inconsequential, ineffective, and trivial. Who wants any of that? If you are not completely without purpose, but are not walking in all you could be, you can become mired in mediocrity.

To rise above the status quo, to operate with your God-given superpowers, to be your very best, you need to know and operate within your purpose. If you don't know why you are here—or you feel like your mission might need some refining—I hope the next few pages help. If you already know what your purpose is, use the following points and suggestions to help others find theirs.

To simplify things, purpose is the *why*. If you haven't seen Simon Sinek's Ted Talk[3] or read his book *Start with Why*,[4] I highly recommend them. Sinek suggests that many people can tell you what they do and how they do it, but they fail to define why they're doing it. He gives examples of individuals and companies who can define what they do and how they do it, but by starting with the "why," they become radically different from their competitors.

Purpose fuels you. It guides your career choices, your extracurricular activities and even the way your personality develops over time. Thinking about it keeps you up at night. Purpose drives you to keep going when your brain tells you to quit. It awakens you and inspires you. It is what helps you to unlock excellence in your personal life and relationships. In your business or workplace. And in the deepest aspects of your personality.

I've discovered my purpose is coming up with creative solutions to problems. I feel most fulfilled when I negotiate a contract, help someone navigate a difficult situation, figure out a clear and accurate way to tell a story, or equip others to make good decisions. I tend to fund charities that help people help themselves, from the Feeding Cabo Kids fishing boat ministry to an anti-trafficking organization in Cambodia that rescues women and teaches them how to design and sew purses from reclaimed fabrics.

My purpose is somewhat harder to peg than others because it operates under the surface in everything I do. It's the common denominator to my passions, not the outward display. And like many other things in life, God doesn't send a neon sign with the answers to our purpose. He wants us to seek purpose—because it forces us to seek Him.

Search Your Soul

You may feel you're not passionate about any one thing. If you could stir up some strong emotions about anything, maybe it would inspire you to do something significant. My search for purpose took this path.

Shortly after my forty-fifth birthday, I struggled with what I wanted to be when I grew up. That's a tough place to be when you have two adult children and you run an international, multimillion-dollar business. But seriously, don't many of us question ourselves and if what we do every day will really matter when we are gone?

My questions lingered in the back of my mind. Meanwhile, to come up with fresh marketing materials for Charlie Bravo Aviation, I registered for a marketing seminar, which turned into something different for me. Instead of the expected corporate messaging seminar, the focus was personal branding.

In a small group setting of all women, the leader asked each of us to identify our character strengths. Then she asked us what characteristics we saw in each person in the group, people we had met only a few hours before. The results were surprising. Each woman learned something new about herself that day. The leader then told us to go home and ask those closest to us what they observed.

I was told I am confident, detail-oriented, honest, discerning, a good manager, and diplomatic. My husband said I was a problem solver. My daughter-in-law told me I don't let conflict simmer.

I reflected on these strengths, along with the things I enjoy in life and work—performing to the best of my ability, having harmony, making others better by being around me, and learning new things.

Then I looked for a common denominator. I like puzzles. I majored in journalism to investigate stories. I love my job when there's a fresh challenge. And voila, the purpose revealed itself, like a gold nugget in a pan of silt and rock.

Interestingly, the same coach who helped me arrive at that conclusion also helped me craft a speech about having to know yourself to really believe in yourself. Sometimes you have to teach something to really understand its implications.

I challenge you to find or hone your purpose. Now. That's what will make the rest of this book a powerful key to flourishing for you. Here's where you can start:

1. Think about your character strengths. Write them down. Don't do it later, do it now. When you list your character strengths, dig deep. I'm not talking about "you're nice," I'm talking about liking who you see when you look in the mirror, which translates to having integrity. You might be funny, but I want you to think about how that benefits others. Does it pull them out of depression or encourage them?

2. Consider what your talents are. The happiest and most successful people in the world are those who have discovered their strengths and talents and put them to use. They somehow seem more alive than the rest of us. Talent is defined as an athletic, creative or artistic aptitude; general intelligence or mental power; the natural endowments of a person. You have talents. And likely, they are God-given. Ask Him to reveal them. Ask others what they see in you. You may have to try new things or take big risks to strike gold. Or your talents may be so ingrained, you don't consciously recognize them.

3. Identify your passions. These can change. Make sure you reassess them regularly. Try new things. Explore. Read. Travel. Find what makes your eyes light up. What you become engrossed in that causes you to lose an entire afternoon. What stirs your heart and soul. Where your convictions are the strongest. What causes you to jump out of bed in the morning? What would you do even for no pay? What brings a smile to your face when you think about it? Passion about something enables us to take it farther than it could go with mere mental or physical human strength. Dictionary.com defines passion as "a strong feeling of enthusiasm or excitement for something or about doing something; the sufferings of Christ between the night of the Last Supper and his death." What would you be willing to die trying to accomplish? Likely that thing lines up with what you are on earth to accomplish.

4. Examine the lists of your strengths, talents, and passions. I can't tell you exactly when the connection will happen, but about this point an underlying theme starts to make itself known. If not, you may have to dig deeper.

My son Jake is passionate about college football. It connects him with people. He played football. He can talk about football intelligently. He can spend an afternoon building a friendship with someone while watching a football game. It's all about relationships for him. Football is merely a conduit that allows him to foster friendships and professional relationships. His purpose is to build meaningful relationships.

Identifying your purpose may require some reflection over a period of time and some analytical thinking. I let it simmer for months but when I finally decided to put pen to paper, it only took a couple of days.

When you figure out what truly awakens you, what keeps you going when things are tough, at what part of the day you get your second wind, and what makes you pump your fist in the air, your purpose will become clear to you, which is a fist-pumping occasion if there ever were one.

Mine crystalized in a speech.

I researched my topic for weeks. I searched my soul for some deep, thought-provoking material. Finally I finished my draft of a keynote speech for college students about rising above the status quo. I agreed to give a speech titled Crushing Mediocrity. I had to crush it on stage.

I rehearsed in front of a mirror and before my accommodating coworkers. I even considered that something could go wrong with the AV and practiced narrating my video clips in my trials. I was prepared.

Approximately 200 young women showed up at Ohio University's 2015 Global Women in Entrepreneurship Day celebration to hear how I succeeded as an entrepreneur against the odds, without any prior experience or training—and after I dropped out of college to have a baby.

Those young women didn't know it was my first speech longer than five minutes. Ever. I delivered the speech without the crowd walking out. The floor didn't open and swallow me whole. I finished with more confidence than when I started. What I didn't anticipate was *the* question.

A pretty engineering student started with a doozy. "What's the hardest thing you've ever done?"

There were lots of things I could have said. Closing my first sale—with a cantankerous client and thirty million dollars. Getting married at twenty-one and staying married for more than twenty-five years and counting. Retaining my sanity with teenagers at home. Maybe even giving the speech I'd just delivered. However, when I really thought about it, I knew the answer.

"Believing in myself."

If I can do it, you can too. Just stand up. Why not here? Why not now? I can promise that if you start, you get stronger as you go. Your confidence will grow. You will know who you are. You will flourish even when the odds are stacked against you.

Use this book. Join my mailing list at renebanglesdorf. com for additional resources and updated information. Internalize the lessons from my life and others who have mentored you. Lean on the scripture that has helped me so much. Know that if you advocate for yourself, if you can resist temptation and make the right choices, if you let go of your anger and hate, you can realize your dreams, no matter what they may be.

You may stumble and fall, but you can always get back up. You can stand up again. You hold that power.

It's time to use it.

About the Author

René Banglesdorf is a conservative business woman in the male-dominated aviation industry. In her day job, she helps some of the world's most successful companies and most influential people buy and sell their private jets. Beyond flight, her passion lies in empowering other outnumbered women to be more confident, enjoy more success and impact their world by finding their voice and using their influence. René and her husband Curt live in the Austin, Texas area, where they enjoy sports, outdoors, and their canine friends.

Endnotes

Chapter 1:

1. Koziarz, Nicki. *Why Her? 6 Truths We Need to Hear When Measuring Up Leaves Us Falling Behind.* B&H Books, March 2018.
2. "Mike Pence doesn't dine alone with other women. And we're all shocked." *Washington Post,* March 30, 2017. Accessed May 20, 2018. https://www.washingtonpost.com/news/the-fix/wp/2017/03/30/mike-pence-doesnt-dine-alone-with-other-women-and-were-all-shocked/?noredirect=on&utm_term=.9d1dc51fbf38
3. "Breaking Through Denial is an Alcoholic's First Step in Recovery," Hazelden Betty Ford (2015). Accessed March 28, 2018. http://www.hazeldenbettyford.org/search?searchTerm=breaking-through-denial-is-first-step-in-recovery-for-alcoholic
4. "New SPLC reports reveal alarming pattern of hate incidents and bullying across country since election," Southern Poverty Law Center. Accessed March 28, 2018. https://www.splcenter.

org/news/2016/11/29/new-splc-reports-reveal-alarming-pattern-hate-incidents-and-bullying-across-country

5. "Political talk is causing problems at work, survey finds," CBS News (2017). Accessed March 28, 2018. https://www.cbsnews.com/news/political-talk-at-work-on-the-job-disruptive-after-election/

Chapter 2:

1. "Bombshell UN Dossier: UN aid workers raped 60,000 people as its claimed organization employs 3,300 paedophiles," *The Sun*, February 13, 2018. Accessed March 29, 2018. https://www.thesun.co.uk/news/politics/5562215/un-aid-workers-raped-60000-people-as-its-claimed-organisation-employs-3300-paedophiles/

2. "Forgiveness," *Psychology Today*. Accessed March 29, 2018. https://www.psychologytoday.com/us/basics/forgiveness

3. Smedes, Lewis B. *Forgive and Forget: Healing the Hurts We Don't Deserve.* HarperOne, 1984.

Chapter 3:

1. "U.S. Weight Loss Market Worth $66 Billion" MarketResearch.com. Accessed March 28, 2018. https://www.prnewswire.com/news-releases/us-weight-loss-market-worth-66-billion-300573968.html

2. "Overweight and Obesity Statistics" National Institute of Diabetes and Digestive and Kidney Diseases. Accessed March 28, 2018. https://www.niddk.nih.gov/health-information/health-statistics/overweight-obesity

3. "35,000 Decisions: The Great Choices of Strategic Leaders," 2015, Roberts Wesleyan College. Accessed March 28, 2018. https://go.roberts.edu/leadingedge/the-great-choices-of-strategic-leaders

4. "Why Should You Limit Your Number of Daily Decisions," Entrpreneur.com, 2015. Accessed March 28, 2018. https://www.entrepreneur.com/article/244395

Chapter 4:

1. Satell, Greg. "What Can We Expect From The Next Decade of Technology?" *Digital Tonto*, July 7, 2013. Accessed March 28, 2018. http://www.digitaltonto.com/2013/what-can-we-expect-from-the-next-decade-of-technology/

2. Christianity Today, 2018. Accessed March 1, 2018. https://www.christianitytoday.com/ct/2018/billy-graham/how-humble-evangelist-billy-graham-changed-christianity.html

Chapter 5:

1. "How Walt Disney, Oprah Winfrey, and 19 Other Successful People Rebounded After Getting Fired," Inc.com. Accessed March 28, 2018. https://www.

inc.com/business-insider/21-successful-people-who-rebounded-after-getting-fired.html
2. Pew Research Center, "The Global Religious Landscape," December 18, 2012. Accessed March 28, 2018. http://www.pewforum.org/2012/12/18/global-religious-landscape-exec/

Chapter 6:

1. "Item 10: I Have a Best Friend at Work," Gallup, 1999. Accessed March 28, 2018. http://news.gallup.com/businessjournal/511/item-10-best-friend-work.aspx
2. Murthy, Vivek. "Work and the Loneliness Epedidemic," *Harvard Business Review*, 2017. Accessed March 28, 2018. https://hbr.org/cover-story/2017/09/work-and-the-loneliness-epidemic
3. "How to Build Employee Trust In An Age Of Short Job Tenures," Fast Company, 2016. Accessed March 28, 2018. https://www.fastcompany.com/3059665/how-to-build-employee-trust-in-an-age-of-short-job-tenures
4. "The Loneliness Epidemic," Christianity Today International, 2014. Accessed March 28, 2018. https://www.todayschristianwoman.com/articles/2014/december-week-3/loneliness-epidemic.html?start=6
5. "The silent tragedy affecting today's children," Your OT, 2017. Accessed March 28, 2018. https://

yourot.com/parenting-club/2017/5/24/what-are-we-doing-to-our-children

6. "There's a Startling Increase in Major Depression Among Teens in the U.S." Time. com, 2016. Accessed March 28, 2018. http://time. com/4572593/increase-depression-teens-teenage-mental-health/

7. "Chasing deadlines and happiness, we forget our lonely elderly," *The Guardian*, 2017. Accessed March 28, 2018. https://www.theguardian.com/ commentisfree/2017/oct/12/chasing-deadlines-and-happiness-we-forget-our-lonely-elderly

8. "Combatting loneliness one conversation at a time," Jo Cox Commission on Loneliness (2017). Accessed March 28, 2018. https://www. jocoxloneliness.org/pdf/a_call_to_action.pdf

Chapter 7:

1. *Zootopia*, Disney Animation Studios (2016). Accessed March 28, 2018. http://www.imdb.com/ title/tt2948356/quotes

2. "ESPN Host Sam Ponder Slams Barstool Sports for Sexist Remarks..." *People*, October 18, 2017. Accessed May 20, 2018. http://people.com/sports/ espn-host-sam-ponder-slams-barstool-sports-sexist-essay-calling-her-slut/

3. "Suicide Among Youth," Centers for Disease Control and Prevention (2017). Accessed March 28, 2018. https://www.cdc.gov/healthcommunication/

toolstemplates/entertainmented/tips/ SuicideYouth.html

4. "NJ students surprise couple with long overdue honeymoon," ABC News, Philadelphia (2017). Accessed March 28, 2018. http://6abc.com/news/ nj-students-surprise-couple-with-long-overdue-honeymoon/2013830/

5. Patterson, Kerry, Grenny, Joseph, McMillan, Ron, Switzler, Al. *Crucial Conversations; Tools for Talking when Stakes are High,* McGraw Hill Education, 2nd edition.

Chapter 9:

1. Duke, Annie, *How I Raised, Folded, Bluffed, Flirted, Cursed and Won Millions at the World Series of Poker,* Hudson Street Press, 2005.

Chapter 10:

1. Warren, Rick. *The Purpose Driven Life: What on Earth Am I Here For?* Zondervan, Expanded Edition, 2013.

2. "Having a Sense of Purpose May Add Years to Your Life," *Association for Psychological Science* (2014). Accessed March 28, 2018. http:// www.psychologicalscience.org/index.php/news/ releases/having-a-sense-of-purpose-in-life-may-add-years-to-your-life.html

3. Sinek, Simon. "How Great Leaders Inspire Action," *TED* (2009). Accessed March 28, 2018. https://

www.ted.com/talks/simon_sinek_how_great_
leaders_inspire_action?language=en#t-2382

4. Sinek, Simon, *Start With Why: How Great Leaders Inspire Everyone to Take Action.* Portfolio; Reprint Edition, December 2011.

Printed in the USA
CPSIA information can be obtained
at www.ICGtesting.com
JSHW082337140824
68134JS00020B/1716